U.S. Department of Justice
Office of Justice Programs
810 Seventh Street N.W.
Washington, DC 20531

John Ashcroft
Attorney General

Deborah J. Daniels
Assistant Attorney General

Sarah V. Hart
Director, National Institute of Justice

Office of Justice Programs
World Wide Web Site
http://www.ojp.usdoj.gov

National Institute of Justice
World Wide Web Site
http://www.ojp.usdoj.gov/nij

Implementing Telemedicine in Correctional Facilities

U.S. Department of Justice–U.S. Department of Defense

Joint Program Steering Group Report

Peter L. Nacci, Ph.D.
National Institute of Justice

C. Allan Turner, D.P.A.
National Institute of Justice

Ronald J. Waldron, Ph.D.
System Planning Corporation

Eddie Broyles
Space and Naval Warfare
Systems Command (SPAWAR)

May 2002
NCJ 190310

National Institute of Justice

Sarah V. Hart
Director

This program was supported under award number 98–IJ–CX–A014 to Tracor, Inc., by the National Institute of Justice, Office of Justice Programs, U.S. Department of Justice. Findings and conclusions of the research reported here are those of the authors and do not reflect the official position or policies of the U.S. Department of Justice.

Reference herein to any specific commercial products, processes, or services by trade name, trademark, or manufacturer, or otherwise does not constitute or imply its endorsement, recommendation, or favoring by the United States Government.

The National Institute of Justice is a component of the Office of Justice Programs, which also includes the Bureau of Justice Assistance, the Bureau of Justice Statistics, the Office of Juvenile Justice and Delinquency Prevention, and the Office for Victims of Crime.

CONTENTS

Executive Summary

An experiment in the late 1990s and an independent evaluation of the experiment determined that providing long-distance health care to inmates is feasible through a system called telemedicine. Telemedicine uses telecommunications equipment that allows health care providers to see and diagnose inmates in prisons located far from health care providers' offices. The experiment showed that prisons could improve inmate health care by providing remote access to more medical specialists while reducing prisoner transport costs and related security management costs.

The National Institute of Justice (NIJ) and Bureau of Prisons, U.S. Department of Justice; and the U.S. Department of Defense cooperated in the experiment. Several Federal prisons with different missions and security levels were connected via a telemedicine network. One of the Federal prisons was a medical center. A Veterans' Administration hospital in Lexington, Kentucky, was also part of the network.

An independent evaluation of the experiment showed that telemedicine could play an important role in delivering quality health care in correctional systems. The costs and benefits vary according to the type and nature of institution requirements, but the costs of telemedicine equipment are continuing to decline. NIJ published a report of the evaluation in 1999 (McDonald, Douglas C., et al., *Telemedicine Can Reduce Correctional Health Care Costs: An Evaluation of a Prison Telemedicine Network*, Washington, DC: U.S. Department of Justice, National Institute of Justice, March 1999, NCJ 175040).

The success of the telemedicine demonstration project led to the decision to use the information from that study to develop a manual on implementing correctional telemedicine. The information in this manual can be used by correctional administrators who are evaluating whether telemedicine is an acceptable approach to providing medical care in their facility.

Planning

The first section guides the reader through the decision process. A medical requirements analysis must be conducted to determine the services currently provided. The satisfaction of the inmates with the current health care services should be evaluated. Alternatives must be evaluated. If telemedicine is selected, an action plan must be developed.

Implementing the Plan

Implementing the plan requires stating the medical requirements in terms of telemedicine. One must know how the telemedicine system will be used in the facility. The performance requirements of the telemedicine system should be determined after careful analysis of state-of-the-art technology. Communications requirements must be determined, then evaluated based on the needs of the facility. Plans for facility requirements and necessary modifications must be made and implemented. Personnel must be recruited and trained for the telemedicine operation.

Evaluating Needs

The technology of telemedicine is unique and must be carefully evaluated and implemented. The hardware, software, and system features that are most cost effective must be identified and implemented. A variety of communication options are available, and these also must be evaluated for cost and capability based on the services to be provided. Space must be identified and, if necessary, modified to meet the needs of telemedicine. Through a careful and thorough planning and contracting process, a successful suite of telemedicine equipment and space can be acquired and installed.

Determining Cost-Benefit

In the final analysis, cost is an important factor. It has been demonstrated that telemedicine can improve services, but in view of the limited funding often provided to correctional facilities, a full cost evaluation should be completed. To further assist in the implementation of telemedicine in corrections, the appendixes contain tools useful for evaluating and planning the costs of a telemedicine program.

Introduction

Purpose

This report provides a model for estimating the relative costs of telemedicine—the provision of health care over a distance using telecommunications technology—under varying conditions in a correctional setting. With the information tools provided in this document, the correctional administrator will be able to determine if telemedicine is a cost-effective option. Information in this report is based on a study of the cost-effectiveness of telemedicine in a correctional system. The companion report, *Telemedicine Can Reduce Correctional Health Care Costs,* should also be consulted for information on estimating the cost of telemedicine. Much of the information included in this report is based on the findings of the March 1999 study. The report is available online at http://www.ncjrs.org/telemedicine/toc.html.

Background

Telemedicine has been under development in the United States for nearly 40 years. In the 1970s and 1980s, the number of telemedicine programs in the United States, Australia, and Canada increased. However, the technologies were expensive, and the programs were often canceled when project funding ceased. Recent technological improvements in equipment and telecommunications have made telemedicine more affordable. As a result, various telemedicine programs are being implemented in the United States and around the world.

Telemedicine is most useful in situations where physical barriers hinder contact between patients and health care providers. Thus it has great potential for use in correctional institutions. Although many U.S. prisons maintain quality health care programs, they usually have only a small number of physicians on staff, and many institutions have only limited access to outside medical specialists. When specialized medical care is required and available, prisoners must be transported outside the secure perimeter of the prison to external medical facilities. Telemedicine allows authorities to improve health care by providing access to more medical specialists, while reducing prisoner transport and related security management costs.

Demonstration Project

In 1994 the U.S. Department of Justice and U.S. Department of Defense signed a Memorandum of Understanding to establish a Joint Program Steering Group (JPSG). The JPSG manages technology development and application programs to enhance the effectiveness of the participants in fulfilling assigned missions. The telemedicine demonstration project, a 3-year effort that concluded at the end of 1998, was part of the JPSG's Biomedical Technology Program. Figure 1 presents the top-level organization of the project.

Objectives. The demonstration project was designed to assess the effect of a correctional telemedicine network in terms of improved prisoner access to specialty health care, lowered security risks, and more reasonable health care costs. Secondary objectives were to identify the practical issues encountered when designing, implementing, and integrating a telemedicine system into an actual prison health care environment and to derive a cost model and develop an informational tool to use when determining the suitability of telemedicine in other applications.

Description and design of the demonstration. The JPSG wanted the project to objectively assess the effectiveness of telemedicine in a prison environment and determine the effect on cost, security, and overall access to health care. The project

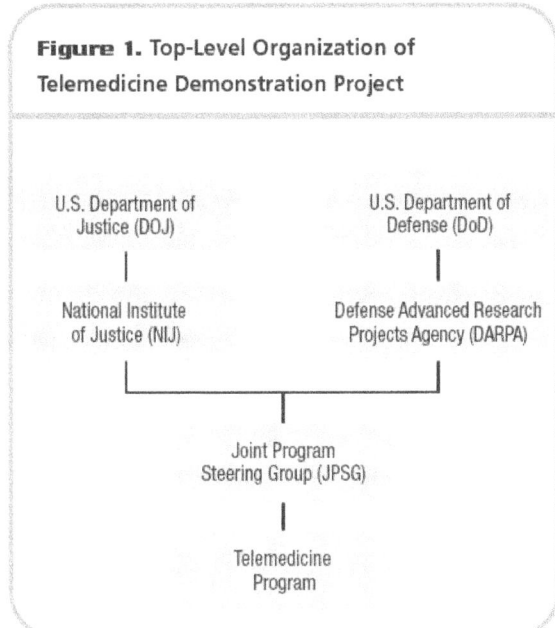

Figure 1. Top-Level Organization of Telemedicine Demonstration Project

U.S. Department of Justice (DOJ)

U.S. Department of Defense (DoD)

National Institute of Justice (NIJ)

Defense Advanced Research Projects Agency (DARPA)

Joint Program Steering Group (JPSG)

Telemedicine Program

included installing a telemedicine network to provide remote medical consultation and electronic medical data transfer. The institutions selected for the demonstration—the U.S. Penitentiary (USP) in Lewisburg and USP–Allenwood (including prisoners from the Federal Correctional Institution (FCI) in Allenwood)—are high-security facilities located in rural Pennsylvania that incarcerate large, aging, long-term inmate populations requiring access to a wide variety of specialized medical care. Both prisons employed consultants to deliver these services in their health care programs. The third site was the Federal Medical Center (FMC) in Lexington, Kentucky, an urban, referral medical center for both medium- and low-security inmates. Both FMC–Lexington and the Veterans' Administration Medical Center (VAMC) in Lexington provided hub site telemedical consultation services for the demonstration. FMC–Lexington was also a remote site because it obtained services from the VAMC. The locations of the facilities used in the demonstration are shown in figure 2.

Telemedicine demonstration system. The telemedicine equipment leased for the project included a PC-based computer workstation with required software, an interactive videoconferencing system with multiple cameras, compatible medical peripheral devices (such as an electronic stethoscope and a micro/intraoral camera), and telecommunications equipment. The various systems were linked via a telecommunications network. A generic telemedicine system is shown in figure 3.

Results

The demonstration showed that telemedicine could play an important role in a quality correctional health care delivery system. The costs and benefits of telemedicine will vary with the type and nature of institution requirements. Based on data from the study, the cost-benefit analysis concluded that a telemedicine consultation would cost an average of $71, compared with $173 for a conventional (face-to-face) health care consultation—a savings of nearly 60 percent. The costs of telemedicine equipment are continuing to decline due to advances in technology, so the costs of telemedicine consultations should also continue to drop.

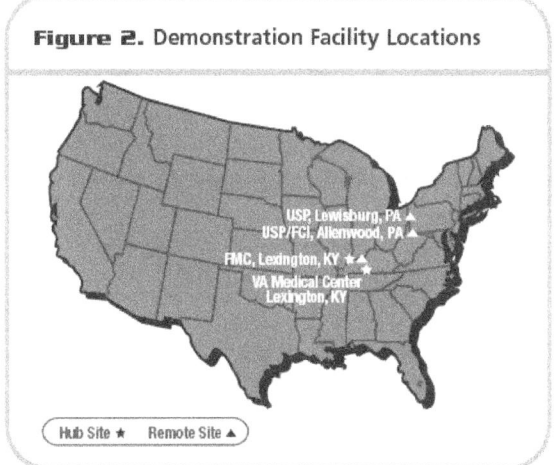

Figure 2. Demonstration Facility Locations

USP, Lewisburg, PA
USP/FCI, Allenwood, PA
FMC, Lexington, KY
VA Medical Center Lexington, KY

Hub Site ★   Remote Site ▲

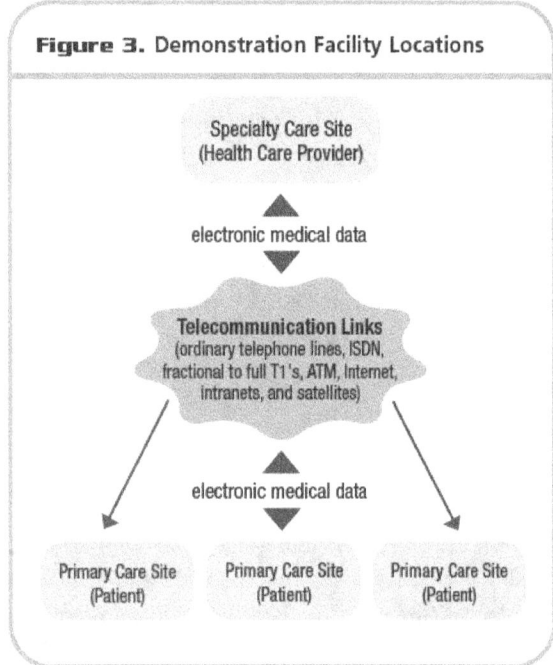

Figure 3. Demonstration Facility Locations

Communications can be one of the most bother-some and expensive aspects of telemedicine operations. Sufficient telecommunications bandwidth is key to the success of telemedicine, and available resources will vary significantly from site to site. In this project, bandwidth on demand was found to be the best technical solution for an operational system and the most economical.

Well-defined participant roles and missions, agreed to in advance, are an integral part of a telemedicine program, and training participants is essential. Up-front training and continuing education should address the specific needs of all participants.

Conclusions

This project demonstrated convincingly that telemedicine can be established within a prison

environment and can be widely embraced by officials and prisoners. Telemedicine was adopted quickly and used frequently in several medical specialty areas. Telemedicine consultations were effective substitutes for in-person consultations in some specialties, particularly psychiatry. Telemedicine also improved some indicators of the quality of care available for prisoners, including the time between referral and actual consultation, the availability of different medical specialists, and access to doctors with more experience in treating prisoners.

Savings from such a program are most likely to result when in-prison consultations by outside contract doctors are replaced by telemedicine consultations. Savings from averted trips to nearby medical facilities are more modest.

An ideal or model telemedicine system—one with all the "bells and whistles"—is not necessary to realize significant cost savings. A simple video teleconferencing system with a close-up camera is adequate for many telemedicine consultations (for dermatology, for example). Document cameras are nice, but a fax machine will usually serve just as well. Electronic stethoscopes were found to be expensive, not often used, and not universally accepted by doctors. Store-and-forward (see appendix H, p. 71) is good technology, but it was not evaluated in this study since personal consultation on interactive video was readily available.

The full report, *Telemedicine Can Reduce Correctional Health Care Costs: An Evaluation of a Prison Telemedicine Network,* demonstrated that correctional agencies can add telemedicine to their medical programs and expect health care costs to decrease.

Implementation
Decision and Planning

The effectiveness of telemedicine as a means of providing health care to a prison population was established in the pilot project. However, each institution, be it a prison or another isolated patient facility, has unique problems and requirements and must determine whether telemedicine can be used effectively in its particular situation. This section discusses the process of deciding whether to implement a telemedicine program in a particular institution. To assist in completing this section, appendix A describes what data and information need to be collected and analyzed. Appendix B contains a list of implementation questions and considerations. Appendix H contains a glossary of terms that will be useful in evaluating telemedicine options.

Implementation Decision Process

Generally, telemedicine is most effective under the following conditions:

- The medical services requirements cannot be effectively met within the facility because—
  - The cost for onsite medical specialists is high.
  - Medical specialists are not available when needed.
  - The small number of requests for specialists does not warrant a contract for outside services.

- The cost to transport patients to outside medical services is very high because—
  - Security requirements demand additional security officers and vehicles.
  - Staff overtime is required for most outside trips.
  - Medical services are distant from the facility.

- Other benefits will accrue from implementing telemedicine, including—
  - Improved safety to security personnel by avoiding the outside transport of high-risk inmates or other detainees.
  - Improved safety to community and medical staff because detainees remain in the institution.
  - Improved quality of medical care.
  - Shorter waiting lists.
  - Improved response time to inmates' medical needs.

To address these and other related issues, a coordinating committee or a decision support group should be assembled to help conduct the review process. This group should include not only policymakers and decisionmakers, but also those who are familiar with the patient population and those medical staff who might be involved in implementing the project. Once the committee is assembled, it can use a simplified decision matrix (figure 4) to evaluate the need for telemedicine capabilities.

Step 1: Conduct a medical requirements analysis. A survey should be conducted in conjunction with other information gathering to determine whether change is required within a facility. If change is indicated, this information will help in designing optimal solutions and evaluating the cost of these options. The following issues should be addressed:

- Evaluate target population demographics:
  - Numbers.
  - Age.
  - Sex.
  - Security threat.
  - Other unusual situations.

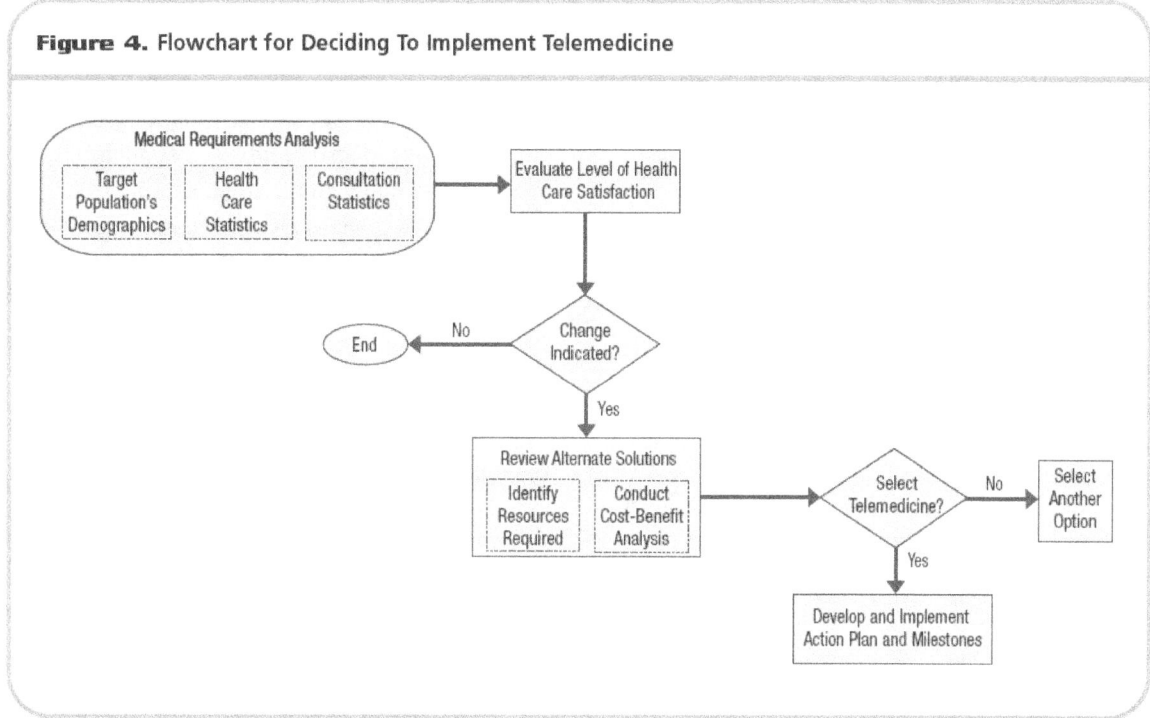

Figure 4. Flowchart for Deciding To Implement Telemedicine

■ Review facility health care statistics:

   ❑ Daily caseload of facility staff.

   ❑ Consultations required or desired.

   ❑ Transfers to outside facilities.

   ❑ Other factors.

■ Evaluate consultation statistics:

   ❑ Types (if any).

   ❑ Frequency (emergency, routine).

   ❑ Waiting time.

   ❑ Location, availability, and qualification of consultants (bilingual?).

   ❑ Time required for consultation.

   ❑ Average cost for visit (internal or external).

   ❑ Supplemental costs (such as security, transportation, etc.).

Step 2: Evaluate level of health care satisfaction within the target population. Besides routine client surveys and health care statistics, indicators of satisfaction or dissatisfaction with the current state of health care within a facility can be gauged in several ways. Health care dissatisfaction may be indicated by—

■ Grievances filed.

■ Inmate complaints to prison administrators, politicians, and media.

■ Inmate refusals of medical treatment by prison medical staff.

■ Legal cases.

■ Surveys of inmate health satisfaction.

Decision: Is change indicated? Any evident problems should be evaluated to determine whether more specialist help is required or if basic medical services need to be augmented. If the information indicates that a change in health care procedures is necessary or desirable, alternative solutions should be evaluated.

Step 3: Review alternate solutions. The data available from the medical requirements analysis (step 1) will indicate the scope of support required. If telemedicine is being considered, the availability and concentration of a cadre of medical specialty providers legally authorized to practice within the facility are important to consider. These providers should be identified and a close working relationship established to help build the program. Other resources that should be identified in order to project a budget and collect sufficient information to complete a cost-benefit analysis include facilities, staff, and equipment.

A preliminary cost-benefit analysis should be conducted prior to undertaking the telemedicine program (or any other solution) to provide necessary information to support requests for budget and program assistance. Through interaction with the medical staff of the health care provider at the hub organization, the facility staff can use data collected in the medical requirements analysis to develop top-level system specifications for vendor surveys of telemedicine hardware and telecommunications interconnects. Cost information can be derived from these surveys. Completing the short form for the cost-benefit analysis (found in appendix C; online at http://www.ojp.usdoj.gov/nij/pubs-sum/190310.htm) may provide sufficient information for preliminary decisionmaking.

Decision: Select telemedicine? Telemedicine is not intended to replace in-facility medical care, but it may supplement in-facility care as needed. If specialist help is indicated, other factors concerning the availability of that help should be evaluated, such as the location and availability of medical specialty support. Other important considerations are the legal, political, and human factor implications of implementing telemedicine in an institution.

Step 4: Develop and implement action plan and milestones. Once the telemedicine program is approved, an action plan and milestones can be prepared. These documents identify the many actions required to implement a successful telemedicine program. Although the schedule is important, several other elements should be addressed, including the types of resources required to complete the action, detailed funding sources for the implementation, and the identity of responsible offices and individuals. It is important that the responsible parties recognize and agree to what is expected of them.

The milestones identified for the project are the significant steps along the path to implementation. For example, preparing the site within the facility where the telemedicine consultations are to take place may consist of several different activities—such as carpentry, electrical work, and environmental control—all of which have scheduled completion dates. Although completing each activity is important, the milestone is the completion of the entire facility to permit installation of the telemedicine hardware. The components of a detailed action plan with milestones are contained in the next section.

Implementation Planning Process

Once the decision has been made to proceed with telemedicine, a carefully orchestrated implementation process is important. With thoughtful planning and attention to detail, a facility should be able to acquire, install, and place in service a telemedicine system without significant problems. The planning described in this section is intended to help develop the action plan and milestones for implementing the program. The interrelationships of the planning tasks are illustrated in figure 5. Unless otherwise noted, these steps are applicable to either hub or remote site planning. Each task in the process is described below. (Some of the detailed surveys may have been completed during the decision process described in the preceding section.)

Define medical requirements. The medical specialties to be provided with telemedicine must be defined before the telemedicine system can be configured. The medical diagnostic needs should have been determined in the medical requirements analysis (step 1 of the implementation decision process described above). The telemedicine system should be configured to meet all current requirements and should allow graceful expansion (adding or modifying system components, rather than replacing them) to accommodate anticipated needs. Appendixes D and E will be helpful in determining medical requirements.

Define telemedicine system usage. Nonmedical aspects of telemedicine must also be defined before the telemedicine system performance can be established. For example, should the system be portable

so it can be operated from multiple locations within the institution? Does it have to interface with or store and transfer medical records? Is store-and-forward capability of video, audio, or data needed? Will the system be used for training? These features may cost money, and additional costs must be justified. Some features, however, may save money.

Define telemedicine system performance requirements. Defining performance requirements is probably the most important step in implementing a telemedicine system. If this assessment is not accurate, the system that is ultimately acquired may fail to meet actual needs or may have costly features and capabilities that are not used.

Follow these general principles:

- Acquire the latest proven technology. Do not buy obsolete goods or become a beta test site for unproven products.

- Make sure training and technical support are adequate—both will be needed.

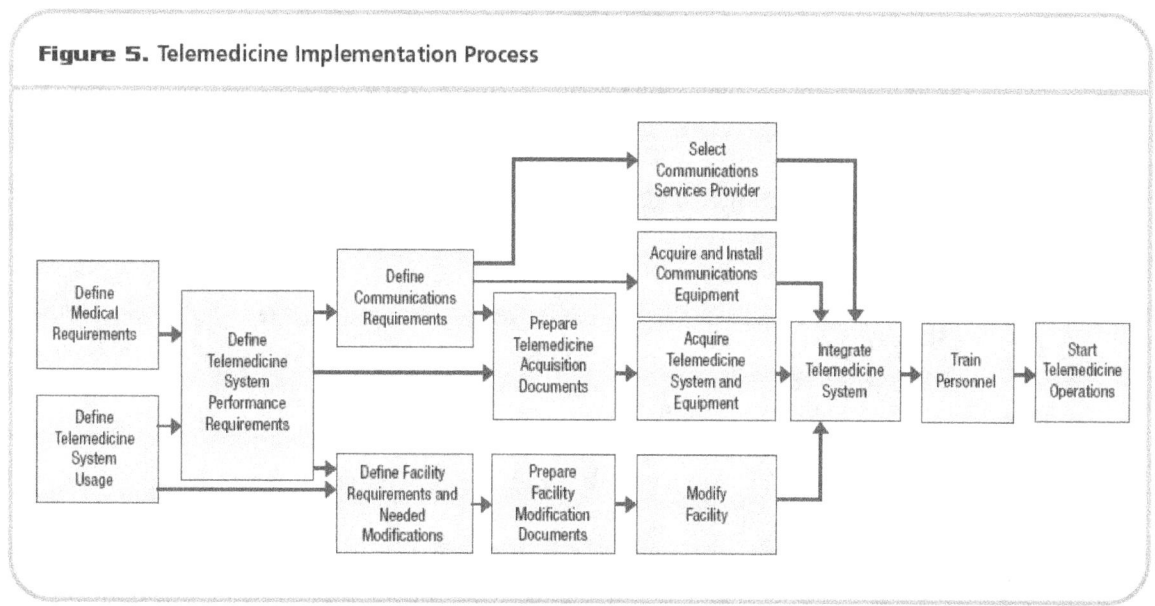

Figure 5. Telemedicine Implementation Process

- Do not acquire a system unless it meets all applicable industry standards, especially those relating to communications compatibility.

Once the basic performance requirements have been defined, the telemedicine system can be configured to provide optimum support. Initially, it should be configured to meet only those requirements (medical specialties) that are most frequently used. Once this baseline system configuration has been established and all associated costs have been defined, it is important to verify equipment needs versus medical needs. The cost-benefit model (see appendix C) can be used to compute the total costs, benefits, and payback period. The procedure should then be repeated for the less frequently used medical specialties, and the cost-benefit recomputed.

Define communications requirements. Defining the communications technology required to provide satisfactory telemedicine system performance at the lowest available cost can be challenging. During the useful life of the system, the communications costs will far exceed the system acquisition costs. The communications requirements depend on the bandwidth needed for each medical specialty and the system utilization time (minutes per month) for each specialty. This utilization pattern can then be evaluated for each communications protocol (switched 56, ISDN, DSL, frame relay, TCP/IP, etc.; see the glossary in appendix H for an explanation of these and other terms). Once this information has been collected, the communications costs can be reviewed with communications services providers.

A different pricing strategy is generally used for the various communications protocols. In addition, the communications services providers may have different pricing strategies, such as discount plans and package deals. The communications costs generally are based on line usage (number of lines times total minutes per line times cost per minute),

or a fixed monthly fee plus line usage, or a fixed monthly fee for a prescribed number of data packets. Because of the different pricing schemes, the communications utilization pattern must be accurately defined to ensure that the least expensive communications protocol has been selected.

Define facility requirements and modifications. The facility modifications that a telemedicine system requires can range from modest to extensive, depending on conditions at the institution. The following descriptions should help planners define the tasks and costs involved in preparing a facility for telemedicine.

- *System location.* Ideally, the telemedicine system should be installed near the health care clinic. The system must be readily accessible both to medical personnel (to save time, especially for accessing medical records and supplies) and to inmates (to save time and costs for inmate movement). Figure 6 depicts possible telemedicine equipment locations.

- *Communications requirements.* Generally, placing the telemedicine room near the telephone demarcation room reduces both equipment and installation costs for communications services. Separating them by great distances can be costly for some communications technologies because of the special equipment needed. (The equipment and communications providers can help determine whether special equipment is needed.) The telemedicine room must be equipped with a telephone in order to set up videoconferences and perform any necessary troubleshooting. A fax machine should be available in the room or nearby.

- *Space requirements.* The telemedicine room must be large enough to accommodate the telemedicine system (allowing adequate viewing distances for cameras and displays) and the personnel who operate it. If the telemedicine room is used for training, additional seating space will be needed. The lighting and HVAC systems of a typical office building should be adequate for telemedicine. In some cases, especially if the floors are not carpeted, acoustic abatement (sound absorption) will be needed. Unless the existing electrical power service is both clean and reliable, a power-line conditioner should be installed to protect the telemedicine equipment from damage caused by power irregularities. The telemedicine room must also be equipped with the furniture, fixtures, and equipment found in a typical doctor's examination room (examination table, sink, x-ray view box, chairs and tables, and various medical supplies).

Prepare telemedicine acquisition documents and facility modification documents. The documents needed depend on the institution's administrative procedures and the implementation or acquisition method chosen. If the major tasks are being subcontracted, a telemedicine system performance specification and statement of work, a drawing package for the facility modification subcontractor, and (probably) drawings and performance specifications for the communication equipment installer will be needed. If the telemedicine system is being implemented by in-house staff, purchase orders must be prepared for each vendor that will be supplying equipment, material, and services.

Select communications services provider. The communications services provider that meets the previously defined requirements at the lowest cost should be selected. To reduce costs, this should be a competitive process.

Acquire and install communications equipment, acquire telemedicine system and equipment, and modify facility. After all modifications and installations are complete, the telemedicine system

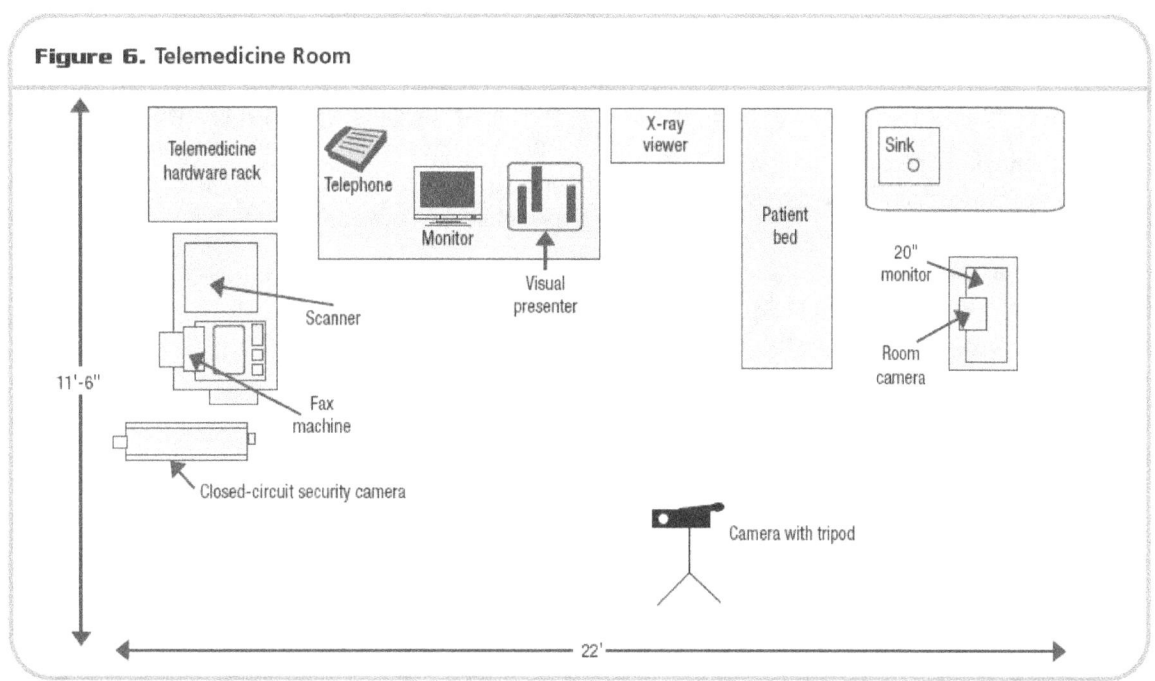

Figure 6. Telemedicine Room

is ready for integration and performance evaluation testing. Complex systems integrating many different components from various manufacturers should be fully integrated at the telemedicine vendor's facility before delivery. This integration testing should reveal most problems at the vendor's facility (where they are easily correctable), rather than at the facility in which the telemedicine system will be implemented (where they are difficult to correct), and should ensure that the equipment meets all requirements. Both the hub and remote systems should be tested using the communications method selected for each, and all performance requirements should be tested under the most realistic conditions achievable. These steps may not be necessary for straightforward installations of what is basically video teleconferencing equipment.

Integrate telemedicine system. After all equipment is installed, the system must be fully integrated and evaluated. All performance parameters should be verified, and all problems should be corrected before the system is accepted. It is extremely important that all integration testing be performed accurately and completely.

Train personnel. All personnel who will operate or maintain the telemedicine system should be thoroughly trained. All users should be able to perform basic operations and troubleshooting; separate personnel are not required for these tasks. Because the medical procedures for conducting telemedicine consultation differ from those used in conventional medicine, training must also encompass these tasks. The demonstration project found that a telemedicine coordinator was essential to the success of the project. Appendix F contains a position description of a telemedicine coordinator.

Operator training is minimal due to the simplicity of the system. Depending on the telemedicine system chosen, the system may be operated in one of two ways:

- With a keyboard or mouse and an on-screen user interface that leads the operator through the required steps.

- With a remote control device (similar to a television remote control) that allows the operator to proceed through the required steps using on-screen cues.

System maintenance training is also minimal because of the self-diagnostic capabilities of the telemedicine system. Most maintenance problems are displayed to the operator. In addition, most systems allow the equipment manufacturer to perform remote diagnostics by dialing into a modem attached to the system and performing additional testing. The failed item can then be exchanged with a replacement item sent by the vendor (assuming the institution has a maintenance agreement with the vendor).

Operators who will use the system for telemedicine consultations require the most intensive training. This training should be planned well in advance of the needed date. Hub personnel and remote site personnel will need different training.

Start telemedicine operations. Once all the previous steps have been successfully completed, the telemedicine system should reliably support all telemedicine needs. Appendix G contains guidance on how to develop procedures for conducting a telemedicine consult.

Technology Evaluation

This section discusses some important issues to consider when selecting a suite of telemedicine equipment that meets the requirements already described. The equipment selection process translates the telemedicine technical performance requirements into hardware and software requirements. The information presented here should be useful in making informed decisions when evaluating and selecting the technological capabilities of a telemedicine system. The intent is to provide guidance in the process, rather than to define the latest telemedicine technology (which is constantly evolving and would soon be obsolete).

By now, the steps described under "Implementation Decision Process" should be completed. This information is needed to identify performance requirements for telemedicine, communications, and facilities. It also helps identify the equipment for which relevant technology information should be reviewed and evaluated.

The technology evaluation process consists of three steps:

1. Determine the required hardware, software, and system features that are most cost effective.

2. Determine the system features needed for making upgrades, expanding performance, or changing requirements.

3. Conduct surveys of hardware, software, and system providers to identify the sources of telemedicine products and the equipment and services offered by each.

The extent to which the implementing organization participates in the technology evaluation process will depend largely on the means chosen to acquire a telemedicine capability:

- If a systems integrator is being used, the integrator should conduct the technology evaluations. In fact, the integrator should maintain current information on the status of each supplier of telemedicine equipment and services and should be able to recommend a system that provides optimum performance to meet requirements and stays within budget.

- If the major telemedicine project tasks are being subcontracted, all potential subcontractors should provide the technology evaluation status of the products they are proposing. Information should be obtained from several candidates so that a variety of equipment from different manufacturers can be compared.

- If all tasks are being performed in-house, each supplier of telemedicine products should be contacted to acquire the technology evaluation data. With an array of manufacturers, products, and technologies to choose from, the system can be configured using the best combination of products and technologies to meet the facility's needs and budget.

More and more institutions are opting for a telemedicine system that is nothing more than a videoconferencing system mounted on top of a monitor, with one specialty camera. Several manufacturers offer videoconferencing systems of this type. Another option is to modify videoconferencing systems for telemedicine applications. The modifications usually involve expanding the interface to accommodate additional cameras and medical devices. These added features may be considered third-party equipment, for which the system vendor does not provide technical or maintenance support and for which no performance guarantees are made. Unless separate agreements have been made with the suppliers of third-party equipment, the implementing institution will likely be responsible for the design, performance, and support of such equipment.

Additional guidance for each technology evaluation area is provided below.

System functions. The telemedicine system should be designed to meet only those medical requirements that are currently needed or that will be needed in the future. However, providing room for upgrades to software and hardware through module replacement can minimize future obsolescence. The telemedicine system must be easy to operate and simple to maintain. All users must be trained to use and maintain the system. If the system is configured properly, user training should require no more than one session of 2 to 4 hours.

Communications. Most innovations in telemedicine technology are occurring in communications. This is also the part of the system that will incur the most cost over its useful life. The communications protocol selected now may not be the most cost-effective solution in the future. Therefore, the cost-benefit analysis should include the option of upgrading communications at a later date.

Computers. Although the versatility and operating speed of computers continue to improve, these improvements should not require constant upgrades to the telemedicine system. The computer should be upgraded only to address additions to system performance requirements or changes to communications protocols. These upgrades can usually be accomplished by adding or replacing modules. Generally, telemedicine systems that do not incorporate medical records or store-and-forward technology will not require a computer.

CODEC. The technology used to transmit telemedicine data is called an analog-to-digital coder/decoder (CODEC). The CODEC should meet all current standards, especially those relating to communications compatibility. Failure to meet all standards could result in incompatibility with other telemedicine systems.

The requirements for a facility's interface between data terminal equipment and data communications equipment (RS–232) should be carefully evaluated. If possible, the data ports on the CODEC should be used for signal and data transmissions. The signals or data are thus transmitted as "in-band" signals and do not require additional communications channels (as opposed to transmitting them "out of band" using separate communications channels). This feature can significantly lower communications costs.

Technological advances have enabled telemedicine equipment designers to incorporate the CODEC and a small video camera into one small, relatively inexpensive unit that sits on top of a video monitor. For many telemedicine programs, this design is adequate to capture many telemedical consultations for considerably less than the cost of a conventional CODEC.

Displays. Telemedicine users consider the display (monitor) to be the most important piece of equipment, because that device provides the visual image viewed by the medical practitioner. The resolution of the display must be adequate for clinical needs, but a larger viewing screen is not necessarily better. The medical users of the system should be consulted before making a final selection. Provisions must be made for maintenance (calibration of colors and alignment) to prevent degradation of display quality. A quality television with a standard high-resolution connector (S-video) is often adequate for telemedicine.

Cameras. The types of cameras needed and their capabilities depend on the medical specialties selected for the system. As with displays, cameras should be selected only after consulting with the medical users of the telemedicine systems. Early systems relied heavily on an expensive "three-chip" camera for adequate video quality. Modern single-chip cameras are much more economical and can provide excellent video quality.

Peripheral medical devices. No specific guidance is provided for selecting peripheral medical devices. The specialty services to be provided to the inmates will determine the peripheral devices needed. The medical staff should be consulted before purchasing this equipment.

Maintenance. Unless the implementing institution has personnel with extensive electronic technical skills, maintenance support should be arranged through system suppliers. The implementers are not likely to experience enough malfunctions to maintain proficiency in system troubleshooting and repair.

Cost Estimation Model

A cost estimation model has been designed to help determine the benefits of applying telemedicine in a particular institution. This model was specifically developed to estimate the costs and benefits of using telemedicine in a prison environment. The results of applying a similar model are discussed in detail in the demonstration project final report. The model described here (and presented in appendix C; online at http://www.ojp.usdoj.gov/nij/pubssum/190310.htm) differs somewhat from the one developed for the demonstration project. Although it follows the computational methods described in the demonstration project report, this version is more straightforward and eliminates the mathematical complexities associated with processing large databases.

The cost-benefit model presented in appendix C is in two forms—simplified and detailed. The simplified model is provided for situations where budgetary estimates are desired or where detailed cost data are not available and must be estimated. The detailed model is presented as a series of eight linked Microsoft® Excel spreadsheets. It allows entry of detailed cost data and should be satisfactory for calculating the costs and benefits of most telemedicine projects. The detailed model can also be tailored to the needs of a particular institution.

The cost-benefit model facilitates comparing the cost of telemedicine acquisition and operation with that of conventional health care. The detailed model allows the following:

- Estimating the cost of any facility modifications that may be needed for telemedicine installation.

- Estimating acquisition costs of the telemedicine system, network and communications equipment, and telemedicine room fixtures.

- Estimating training costs.

- Estimating the cost to operate and maintain the telemedicine system.

- Estimating the cost to provide medical personnel to conduct the medical consultations.

- Estimating the medical cost savings that accrue by replacing conventional medical care with telemedicine.

- Estimating the transportation cost savings that accrue by replacing conventional medical care with telemedicine.

- Calculating the annual cost savings that accrue from telemedicine acquisition and operation, the period required for the savings to pay back the telemedicine acquisition cost, and the annual savings that continue to accrue after payback of telemedicine acquisition cost.

Appendix A

Areas of Inquiry for the Medical
Requirements Analysis

This appendix provides sample areas of inquiry useful in conducting a medical requirements analysis. The analysis is useful in defining the clinical and health care requirements of an institution to ensure a good fit between the telemedicine system design and end-user needs.

The methodology for the analysis includes interviews with medical and administrative staff to identify the medical consultative and diagnostic requirements for each specialty area and to gain familiarity with the medical operations and prisoner-patient issues. Surveys can be administered and statistics compiled on the volume and frequency of internal and external medical consultations (i.e., visits to the prisons by medical consultants and trips to local medical facilities, respectively) and numbers of prisoners on waiting lists. From these statistics, the telemedicine opportunities, clinic requirements, and other telemedicine capabilities (e.g., mode of interaction, type of information that would be transferred during a consultation, resolution requirements, medical peripheral devices) can be determined. The analysis also shows the areas with the greatest medical needs.

The medical requirements analysis is important for two reasons. First, it helps ensure that the technology system procured will suit the medical needs of the organization. Second, it educates the staff on telemedicine, helps develop a rapport between the project team and telemedicine site staff, and fosters local site support for the program.

Prison Demographics

- Location.
  - Environment.
  - Security level.

- Prison population.
  - Total number.
  - Population statistics.
    - —Age.
    - —Gender.
- Prison health clinic statistics.
  - Daily case load (average).
  - Daily case load.
    - —Percent handled by in-house medical staff.
    - —Percent handled by outside consultants.
  - Specialty areas (specify).
    - —Percent handled by in-house medical staff.
    - —Percent handled by outside consultants.
  - Case types (specify).
    - —Percent handled by in-house medical staff.
    - —Percent handled by outside consultants.
  - Consultations.
    - —Percent handled by in-house medical staff.
    - —Percent handled by outside consultants.
  - Percent transferred to medical centers for consultations.
- Medical staff.
  - Positions.
  - Required credentials or training levels.
  - Organizational structure.

Onsite Biomedical Technology and Capabilities

List existing features.

Medical Applications: Statistics

- External consultations (the inmate must leave the facility).
  - Outpatient (local).
    - Specialty area.
    - Type cases.
    - Routine versus emergency—percent of total external consultations.
    - Frequency of consultations (in clinics and on-demand).
    - Location of consultations.
    - Costs of consultations.
    - Percent of total consultations appropriate for telemedicine.
    - Time required per consultation (average).
    - Data required.
    - Static or dynamic images, textual.
    - Source of data (x-ray, EKG strip, etc.).
    - Frequency of data production and transmission.
    - Frequency of data recalled for later use.
    - Format of data for presentation (color, hard copy, etc.).
    - Response time for data transmission.
    - Equipment used during consultation.
    - Number of prisoners on waiting list.
    - Factors causing waiting list.
    - Total number of outpatient consultations.
    - Total estimated hours.
    - Medical operational procedures for consultations.
  - Inpatient (local).
    - Specialty area.
    - Type cases.
    - Routine versus emergency—percent of total external consultations.
    - Frequency of consultations (in clinics and on-demand).
    - Location of consultations.
    - Costs of consultations.
    - Percent of total consultations appropriate for telemedicine.
    - Time required per consultation (average).
    - Data required.
    - Static or dynamic images, textual.
    - Source of data (x-ray, EKG strip, etc.).
    - Frequency of data production and transmission.
    - Frequency of data recalled for later use.
    - Format of data for presentation (color, hard copy, etc.).
    - Response time for data transmission.
    - Equipment used during consultation.
    - Number of prisoners on waiting list.
    - Factors causing waiting list.
    - Total number of inpatient consultations.
    - Total estimated hours.
    - Medical operational procedures for consultations.
- Internal consultations (in prison).
  - Specialty area.
  - Type cases.
  - Routine versus emergency—percent of total internal consultations.
  - Frequency of consultations (in clinics and on-demand).
  - Location of consultations.
  - Costs of consultations.
  - Percent of total consultations appropriate for telemedicine.
  - Time required per consultation (average).
  - Data required.

❏ Static or dynamic images, textual.

❏ Source of data (x-ray, EKG strip, etc.).

❏ Frequency of data production and transmission.

❏ Frequency of data recalled for later use.

❏ Format of data for presentation (color, hard copy, etc.).

❏ Response time for data transmission.

❏ Equipment used during consultation.

❏ Number of prisoners on waiting list.

❏ Factors causing waiting list.

❏ Total number of internal consultations.

❏ Total estimated hours.

❏ Medical operational procedures for consultations.

■ Relocations to outside medical centers (Transfers: The inmate must be removed from the facility for treatment, and he/she may be transferred for an indefinite stay at another prison hospital with broader health care capabilities, or he/she may be transferred to a private hospital.).

❏ Frequency of transfers in each specialty area.

❏ Medical costs.

❏ Transportation costs.

❏ Administrative and overhead costs.

❏ Percent of total consultations appropriate for telemedicine.

Appendix B
Telemedicine Review and
Implementation

This appendix provides a list of considerations to review before implementing a telemedicine program. The list has been developed in coordination with the implementation planning process described in the main section of this report.

The appendix is intended to give guidance in considering those factors involved in implementing a telemedicine program. In this sense, it is a reminder to consider and evaluate all technical, performance, and cost areas so the institution can acquire the telemedicine system that best meets its needs. Thus, this list duplicates some information found in other parts of the report.

Implementing a telemedicine system is usually an iterative process. As you proceed through the required steps, you will need to reevaluate prior steps to ensure that the decisions made are still the best choices. You may determine that previous choices must be changed and the succeeding steps repeated.

Can Telemedicine Satisfy Your Institutional Requirements?

■ Can telemedicine save money? This is often the most difficult question to answer in advance. The cost-benefit analysis conducted for the telemedicine demonstration project[1] clearly shows that telemedicine can save money for facilities similar to the demonstration project. Completing the cost-benefit model in appendix C will help answer this question for your facility.

■ Can telemedicine provide better health care? If access to health care is limited because of a remote location, limited availability of nearby health services, excessive costs of local health care, security concerns, or contractual or administrative restrictions, telemedicine can often be especially beneficial. Telemedicine usually provides more accessible medical care where local conditions restrict access to physicians or medical facilities.

■ Can telemedicine reduce liability? If telemedicine is used correctly, it may reduce medical liability by making medical services more readily available and by fully documenting (through audio or video recording) the medical consultations of sensitive cases.

■ How will telemedicine affect inmate management?

■ Which organizations (departments) should be involved in implementing and using telemedicine?

■ What resources are available for implementing telemedicine (resources within your facility that have sufficient time to devote to telemedicine acquisition)?

  ❑ Management.

  ❑ Contractual.

  ❑ Financial.

  ❑ Technical.

■ Based on the resources available, which acquisition method should be used?

  ❑ Contract the tasks to a full-service organization.

  ❑ Manage the project, but subcontract major tasks.

  ❑ Perform the acquisition and installation tasks using in-house resources.

■ What type of contract (or interagency agreements) will be required to establish the remote-hub working relationships?

---

1. See *Telemedicine Can Reduce Correctional Health Care Costs: An Evaluation of a Prison Telemedicine Network,* a report by the U.S. Department of Justice, National Institute of Justice, Washington, D.C., March 1999, NCJ 175040.

- Who schedules consultations? What are the logistics of scheduling consultations, resolving schedule conflicts, and handling emergencies?

- How will cost invoicing and reimbursement be managed?

Define Medical Requirements

- Which medical specialties and subspecialties are required to meet current health care needs?

- Can telemedicine serve the medical diagnostic requirements for the specialties and subspecialties needed?

- Will the telemedicine system use rate be sufficient to justify its acquisition (i.e., how many consultations per specialty per month would be conducted using telemedicine)?

- Remote-site issues: Where will the hub site be located? Can it support our health care needs at the required utilization rate? What are the individual (or per hour) consultation costs for each medical specialty?

- Hub-site issues: Will we be working with one or many remote sites? Will there be enough (or too many) requests for consultations for each specialty?

Define Telemedicine System Usage (Both Medical and Nonmedical Applications)

- In addition to medical consultations, what will the telemedicine system be used for?

  - Inmate counseling (social, psychiatric, medical).

  - Training of inmates or staff.

  - Medical training and recertification of health services personnel.

  - Arraignment.

  - Judicial proceedings.

  - Video conferences (prison staff).

  - Attorney-inmate conferences.

- From how many locations within the facility must the telemedicine system be accessible?

  - One (fixed system location).

  - More than one (portable system or multiple systems).

- Will the telemedicine system be integrated (initially or in the future) with our local area network or wide area network, or should it be separate?

- Will the telemedicine system be used to generate, transfer, or maintain medical records or administrative data?

- Will the telemedicine system be integrated with medical or administrative systems?

- Will remote (not located in the telemedicine room) consoles be needed to view the consultations or examine records?

- Should the telemedicine system have a store-and-forward capability, or should the consultations be interactive? If the former, which store-and-forward capabilities are needed?

  - High-definition video still images.

  - Video clips.

  - Audio clips.

  - VCR recordings.

  - Data files (medical or administrative records).

  - Storage devices (type and capacity).

- Should the telemedicine system incorporate radiology?

Define Telemedicine System Performance Requirements

This task translates the medical and other system usage requirements into performance requirements for the telemedicine system. If you are employing a full-service contractor or are subcontracting the major implementation tasks, the contractor should help you prepare a performance specification for a telemedicine system that is appropriate for your needs. If you are performing all tasks in house, you must determine the performance requirements for the hardware and software that you need. This is not as difficult as it may seem, because several vendors sell videoconferencing or telemedicine systems that are already integrated and may meet most of your needs. You may have to add third-party equipment to complete your system.

Once you know the telemedicine system performance requirements, you can research which available products meet your needs. Use the Internet and trade magazines to locate vendors offering the products and services. You can often download the necessary technical, availability, and cost data from the Internet. Otherwise, contact the vendor directly for the necessary information.

Now you are ready to configure the telemedicine system that best meets your needs and budget from the array of available products and services.

Define Communications Requirements

Based on the information developed thus far, you should know the types of medical consultations to be performed each month, the estimated time (minutes per month) online with each medical specialty, and the communications bandwidth necessary for each specialty. Now you need to determine which communications protocols are available at your location. Consider the following (see glossary at appendix H for details):

- Switched 56.

- Integrated services digital network (ISDN).

- Digital subscriber line (DSL).

- Asynchronous transfer mode (ATM).

- Frame relay.

- Transmission control protocol (TCP)/Internet protocol (IP).

Your selection of communications protocols may be limited because—

- An existing protocol must be used at your facility.

- You must match the protocol used by a remote site.

- The desired protocol may not be available at your location.

When selecting the communications protocol, you must consider any unusual conditions that may exist at your facility. Since most communications services providers will terminate the communications lines in the telephone demarcation room, your proximity to the demarcation room may influence your selection of protocols. Carefully evaluate communications performance if the telemedicine system must be operated from multiple locations or if the distance from the telemedicine room to the demarcation room requires the electrical signals to be converted and transmitted over a fiber-optic cable.

Define Facility Requirements and Needed Modifications

Facility modifications can range from none to extensive. Usually, older facilities require more extensive modifications than newer ones.

- Location considerations.
  - Near communications facilities.
  - Near medical records.
  - Easily accessible by medical staff.
  - Conveniently located for patients (if remote site).
  - In a quiet area without background noise.
  - Security can be maintained and not compromised.

- Configuration considerations.
  - Room shape allows proper placement of equipment and fixtures.
  - For jails and prisons, inmate examination area allows egress route for medical personnel.
  - Space is available for auxiliary seating if equipment or room is used for training, videoconferences, or visitors.
  - Ingress and egress do not require patients to cross over cables or interfere with camera views and do not allow them to tamper with equipment.
  - For jails or prisons, doors are not lockable from inside. (Doors should be locked when the telemedicine system is not in use.)

- Lighting.
  - Adequate lighting, evenly distributed, without glare or shadows.
  - Variable light intensity (desirable—not required).

- Acoustics: Most rooms require some type of acoustic treatment for good audio performance. There should be no distracting background noises. This is critical when using electronic stethoscopes (at both hub and remote sites). Confidential med-

ical discussions should not be audible outside the telemedicine room. Treating acoustic problems generally proceeds in the following order:
  - Carpet the floor.
  - Insulate the ceiling, especially if a suspended ceiling is used.
  - Insulate the walls.
  - Install sound absorption on the walls.

- Electrical.
  - 110-volt, 15-ampere service is adequate for most systems.
  - An uninterruptible power supply (UPS) is not normally required, but is highly desirable. If your facility experiences frequent power outages, voltage drops or surges, or spikes on the power line, a UPS is essential.

- HVAC: The temperature and environmental controls of a typical office building are satisfactory. Additional HVAC may be needed for training or videoconference equipment.

Prepare Telemedicine Acquisition Documents

The specific acquisition documents needed will depend on your administrative procedures and the acquisition method chosen.

- Administrative documents.

- Contracts, subcontracts, purchase orders.

- Statements of work.

- System performance specifications.

- Technical specifications for equipment.

- Testing procedures, both factory acceptance and onsite acceptance.

- Maintenance and support agreements.

- Shipping instructions.

Prepare Facility Modification Documents

If facility modifications are required (and especially if they are to be subcontracted), all modifications should be described in documents that are standard to building practices in your area for the building trades involved. As a rule, the documentation formats established by the American Institute of Architects should be followed.

Most facilities require approval of the facility manager before any modifications are permitted. After the facility is modified, the building drawings and specifications should be updated to the "as-built" conditions:

- Building or modification permit (if required by local code or regulations).

- Drawings or specifications (for each building trade to be subcontracted).

- Inspection records.

Select Communications Services Provider

Sometimes selection of the communications services provider is controlled by conditions outside the telemedicine project:

- Your organization already has a service agreement with a particular provider.

- Operation with the hub (or remote) site restricts your choices.

- Other users of the communications services may affect your decision.

Unless there is some overriding reason to the contrary, the communications services provider should be selected based on lowest cost. However, lowest cost is sometimes difficult to determine, because each service provider has different cost structures. If available, your expected communications utilization pattern should form the basis for cost comparisons.

Acquire and Install Communications and Telemedicine System Equipment; Modify the Facility

All these tasks should be accomplished on the basis of documents developed earlier. You will need to maintain cost and schedule control during this period to avoid exceeding your budget or missing deadlines.

Integrate the Telemedicine System

Your telemedicine system should be integrated twice: first at the system integrator's facility (or at your facility if you are integrating the system) and again after the system is installed. This step assumes that you are acquiring both hub and remote systems.

The systems should be fully integrated and all performance parameters verified while the systems are at the same location. System performance can be verified and problems resolved more efficiently and with a smaller technical staff if all parties can witness the performance of both the hub and remote systems. If possible, during testing at the system integrator's facility, use the same communications methods and protocols that will be used for the final installation, even to the extent of transmitting the signals outside your facility in a loopback configuration.

After the hub and remote systems have been installed onsite, the integration tests previously performed should be repeated. (The difficulty of resolving any remaining problems will quickly illustrate the value of the previous integration testing.) If the integration testing is performed thoroughly and all problems are corrected, you should not experience any major technical problems when operating your telemedicine system.

Train Personnel

Conduct training in accordance with training plans. If possible, training should be conducted onsite, using the actual telemedicine system implemented for your program. All personnel using telemedicine for the first time should be permitted an additional period of hands-on operation to thoroughly familiarize themselves with their new tasks.

Start Telemedicine Operations

Congratulations! You have now completed the telemedicine acquisition process. You will probably be surprised how quickly everyone adapts to telemedicine and takes advantage of all the benefits it provides.

Appendix C
Telemedicine Cost-Benefit Model

The cost-benefit model presented in this appendix allows you to calculate the cost of acquiring a telemedicine system, the fiscal savings you can expect from using such a system, and other cost-benefit values. Two models are provided: a simplified model for initial cost evaluation and budget planning and a detailed model for calculating more precise and comprehensive costs based on estimates received from material providers, equipment suppliers, and subcontractors; telemedicine system operating costs; and financial savings that accrue from using telemedicine. The simplified cost estimation model is a single page, whereas the detailed model is eight pages. (In electronic form, these pages are linked spreadsheets.)

The cost models used in this report were developed using Microsoft® Excel; however, other commercial spreadsheets would be suitable for this purpose. Electronic copies of the spreadsheets used in this report are available online at http://www.ojp. usdoj.gov/nij/pubs-sum/190310.htm. The embedded formulas in the electronic copies are not detailed in this summary. The reader is strongly encouraged to download electronic copies of the model spreadsheets and become familiar with the formulas.

In both models, highlighted cells have been protected and do not permit data entry (without password), to prevent inadvertent alteration of the model. These cells either require no data entry or contain equations. Results will be presented in the highlighted cells when sufficient data have been entered in the nonhighlighted cells to allow the models to complete the calculations. Provisions have not been made in the models for accumulating total medical costs within an institution for either telemedicine or conventional health care. The following types of information should not be entered into the models: costs common to both telemedicine and conventional health care (e.g., medical records update and maintenance) and costs

for those conventional medical practices not addressed by telemedicine (e.g., invasive medical procedures).

Simplified Cost Estimation Model

The Simplified Cost Estimation Model is presented in figure C–1. The model is divided into the following categories and subcategories.

- Costs incurred by telemedicine.
  - Capital cost.
  - Operating cost.
  - Medical personnel cost.
- Costs avoided by telemedicine.
  - Medical personnel cost.
  - Patient escort and transportation cost.
- Other telemedicine system uses.
- Telemedicine costs and benefits.

Costs incurred by telemedicine

These are costs for acquiring and placing in service all capital assets, the cost of operating and maintaining the telemedicine system, and the cost of medical services.

Capital cost. The total cost of each capital asset is to be entered in the cells provided. Suggested values for the service life of each asset have been entered; however, you can change these if desired by overwriting the cell values. The model will calculate the total capital cost, as well as the cost per year. Straight-line depreciation, without salvage value, is assumed.

- *Installation.* Enter the cost of all modifications and improvements needed to prepare the facility telemedicine room. Some facilities may require

Figure C–1. Simplified Cost Estimation Model

COSTS INCURRED BY TELEMEDICINE				
CAPITAL COST		LIFE (yr)	TOTAL COST	COST/YEAR
Installation		20		
Telemedicine System		10		
Network/Communications Equipment		10		
Telemedicine Room Fixtures		10		
Training		5		
Total Capital Cost				
OPERATING COST		HRS/MO	$/MONTH	COST/YEAR
Telemedicine System Operation				
Communications				
Maintenance/Support				
Total Operating Cost				
MEDICAL PERSONNEL COST	MIN/CONSULT	CONSULTS/YR	$/CONSULT	COST/YEAR
Psychiatry				
Dermatology				
Orthopedics				
Other				
Total Medical Personnel Cost				
Total Cost Incurred				

COSTS AVOIDED BY TELEMEDICINE				
MEDICAL PERSONNEL COST		CONSULTS/YR	$/CONSULT	COST/YEAR
Internal Consultations				
External Consultations				
Medical Center Consultations				
Other Medical Cost				
Total Medical Personnel Cost				
PATIENT ESCORT/TRANSPORT COST		ESCORTS/YR	$/ESCORT	COST/YEAR
Internal Consultation—Escort Labor/Other Cost				
External Consultation—Escort Labor/Other Cost				
External Consultation—Transport Cost				
Medical Center—Escort Labor/Other Cost				
Medical Center—Transport Cost				
Total Patient Escort/Transport Cost				
Total Cost Avoided by Telemedicine				

continued . . .

. . . continued from page 37

OTHER TELEMEDICINE SYSTEM USES			
TELEMEDICINE SYSTEM USE	**HOURS/MONTH**	**COST/YEAR**	**$ SAVED/YR**
Inmate Counseling			
Training of Inmates or Staff			
Medical Training/Recertification			
Arraignment of Inmates			
Judicial Proceedings			
Attorney–Inmate Conferences			
Staff Video Conferences			
Other			
Total Cost of Other Uses of Telemedicine System			

TELEMEDICINE COSTS AND BENEFITS			
Total Cost/Year Incurred by Telemedicine		Total Consultations/Year	
Total Cost/Year Avoided by Telemedicine		Cost/Consultation	
Cost Adjustment for Other System Uses		Cost Savings/Consultation	
Total Cost Savings/Year		Cost Savings/Year (After Payback)	
Cost Payback Period (Months)			

no changes, while others may require extensive changes. (Refer to the worksheet in the detailed cost model for an explanation or breakdown of costs if more information is needed.)

- *Telemedicine system.* Enter the acquisition cost of the telemedicine system, assuming that it is purchased and installed as an integrated system. Otherwise, enter the total cost of all equipment, plus the labor cost of integration. Include the cost of installing and testing the telemedicine system.

- *Network/communications equipment.* Enter the cost of any equipment required to connect your telemedicine system with your communications services provider. Examples of equipment in this category include inverse multiplexers, fiber-optic converters, and communication cables.

- *Telemedicine room fixtures.* Enter the cost of everything needed in the telemedicine room, except the telemedicine system itself. Examples include table, chairs, telephone, fax machine, and file cabinet.

- *Training.* Enter the cost of training operations and maintenance personnel as well as medical staff. As a rule, the telemedicine system supplier provides training on operating and maintaining the equipment. Training may also be required for medical personnel who present the patient (inmate) to the physician during the telemedicine consultation. The training considered here is the one-time initial training for starting the telemedicine project; as such, it is a capital cost. Training conducted in the future, as part of the day-to-day operations, would be an operating cost.

Operating cost. The operating cost includes all expenses associated with running the telemedicine system.

- *Telemedicine system operation.* Enter the cost per month of maintaining the telemedicine room (but not the telemedicine system). Note: The hours per month of telemedicine system operation, which is not used in the calculations, will be automatically computed and is the same as the hours per month of communications.

- *Communications.* Enter the cost of all communications unique to the telemedicine system. (Refer to the telemedicine operating cost spreadsheet in the detailed model for an example of the types of costs to include.) The hours per month of communications is calculated based on the minutes per consultation and the number of consultations entered in the medical personnel cost section (see below). It is for information purposes only and is not used in calculating the communications cost.

- *Maintenance/support.* Enter all costs associated with maintaining the telemedicine system in good working order. This includes labor for troubleshooting and repair, spare parts, and any items needed for periodic maintenance. If you purchase a maintenance contract, enter the cost of the contract.

Medical personnel cost. The cost of the medical staff involved with telemedicine is entered in this section. The cost entered must be carefully considered to achieve an accurate comparison with the cost of conventional care. For each medical specialty to be practiced using telemedicine, enter the number of consultations per year and the cost per consultation. Also, enter the time (in minutes) that each consultation is expected to take.

Once you have entered all the information requested above, the model will calculate the total cost per year incurred by telemedicine.

Costs avoided by telemedicine

Medical personnel cost. Enter the cost of medical staff that would have been incurred in the absence of telemedicine. This cost may be either for staff salary or for payment of medical fees to contract service providers. For each type of consultation shown, enter the number of consultations per year that telemedicine replaced and the cost of each consultation. The cost per consultation includes both the physician's cost and the cost of any other

staff members needed to accompany or assist the physician.

- *Internal consultations.* Enter the cost of medical consultations for which, in the absence of telemedicine, a physician would have provided medical care within the institution.

- *External consultations.* Enter the cost of treatments patients would have received at a nearby medical facility in the absence of telemedicine.

- *Medical center consultations.* Enter the cost of treatments patients would have received at a medical center located a considerable distance from the institution. Remember that in such cases, the patient usually remains at the medical center, perhaps for an extended period of time.

Patient escort and transport cost. Enter the cost that would have been incurred in escorting and transporting a patient, either inside or outside the institution, for medical care. The labor costs include all institution staff involved in the escort or transport. The transport costs include all nonlabor costs that would have been incurred in the escort or transport. Enter cost data for the internal, external, and medical center consultations. Note that the information to be entered here is the number of escorts or transports avoided, which is not the same as the number of medical consultations.

Other telemedicine system uses

If the telemedicine system is to be used for purposes other than providing medical services, an appropriate credit should be made against the telemedicine system capital and support cost. Based on the hours per month of other uses, the model will calculate the cost per year for the other uses and for the cost savings to be credited to telemedicine.

Telemedicine costs and benefits

Once you have entered all the information requested above, the model will calculate the costs and

Figure C–2a. Detailed Cost Estimation Model—Telemedicine Cost-Benefit Summary

COSTS INCURRED BY TELEMEDICINE				
CAPITAL COST		**LIFE (yr)**	**TOTAL COST**	**COST/YEAR**
Installation				
Telemedicine System				
Network/Communications Equipment				
Telemedicine Room Fixtures				
Training				
Total Capital Cost				
OPERATING COST		**HRS/MO**	**$/MONTH**	**COST/YEAR**
Telemedicine System Operation				
Communications				
Maintenance/Support				
Total Operating Cost				
MEDICAL PERSONNEL COST	**MIN/CON (Avg)**	**CONSULTS/YR**	**$/CONSULT (Avg)**	**COST/YEAR**
Psychiatry				
Dermatology				
Orthopedics				
Other Medical Cost				
Total Medical Personnel Cost				
Total Cost Incurred by Telemedicine				
COSTS AVOIDED BY TELEMEDICINE				
MEDICAL PERSONNEL COST		**CONSULTS/YR**	**$/CONSULT(Avg)**	**COST/YEAR**
Internal Consultations				
External Consultations				
Medical Center Consultations				
Total Medical Personnel Cost				
PATIENT ESCORT/TRANSPORT COST		**ESCORTS/YR**	**$/ESCORT**	**COST/YEAR**
Internal Consultation—Escort Labor/Other Cost				
External Consultation—Escort Labor/Other Cost				
External Consultation—Transport Cost				
Medical Center—Escort Labor/Other Cost				
Medical Center—Transport Cost				
Total Patient Escort/Transport Cost				
Total Cost Avoided by Telemedicine				

continued . . .

. . . continued from page 40

OTHER TELEMEDICINE SYSTEM USES			
TELEMEDICINE SYSTEM USE	**HOURS/MONTH**	**COST/YEAR**	**$ SAVED/YR**
Inmate Counseling			
Training of Inmates or Staff			
Medical Training/Recertification			
Arraignment of Inmates			
Judicial Proceedings			
Attorney–Inmate Conferences			
Staff Video Conferences			
Other			
Total Cost of Other Uses of Telemedicine System			

TELEMEDICINE COSTS AND BENEFITS			
Total Cost/Year Incurred by Telemedicine		Total Consultations/Year	
Total Cost/Year Avoided by Telemedicine		Cost/Consultation	
Cost Adjustment for Other System Uses		Cost Savings/Consultation	
Total Cost Savings/Year		Cost Savings/Year (After Payback)	
Capital Cost Recovery Period			

benefits, as well as other information that may be useful when considering telemedicine acquisition.

Detailed Cost Estimation Model

The concept for the detailed cost estimation model is the same as that for the simplified model. The model is organized with the summary sheet listed first and the more detailed sheets following, as shown in figures C–2a through C–2h. Entry of data proceeds from the last sheet forward. This format was chosen to allow management to review the results starting at the top and working toward the more detailed information.

Telemedicine cost-benefit summary

The Telemedicine Cost-Benefit Summary (figure C–2a) is identical to that used for the simplified cost estimation model. However, in this case, all information is calculated from data entered on the detail sheets. Only the hours per month for other uses of

the telemedicine system (as described previously) need to be entered.

Capital cost

The Capital Costs sheet (figure C–2b) can be used alone or in conjunction with the Telemedicine Installation Worksheet (figure C–2g) or the Telemedicine Equipment Worksheet (figure C–2h) or both. If you are using the electronic version, data entered on either of these worksheets will automatically be transferred to the Capital Costs sheet. The worksheet calculates the amortization (depreciation) of all capital assets. Straight-line depreciation is used; however, if another method is desired, Excel offers several alternative means of calculating depreciation.

Telemedicine operating costs

The Telemedicine Operating Costs sheet (figure C–2c) is used to accumulate all costs to operate and maintain the telemedicine system, except for the cost of medical personnel.

Figure C–2b. Detailed Cost Estimation Model—Capital Costs

COST CATEGORY	LABOR			EQUIP/MTRL		OTHER COST	TOTAL COST	AMORTIZATION		
	HOURS	RATE	COST	COST	SHIP			LIFE	SALVAGE	COST/YR
INSTALLATION										
From Telemed Install Worksheet										
Total Installation Cost										
TELEMEDICINE SYSTEM										
From Telemed Equip Worksheet										
Total Telemedicine System Cost										
NETWORK/COMM EQUIP										
From Telemed Equip Worksheet										
Total Network/Comm Eq Cost										
TELEMEDICINE ROOM FIXTURES										
From Telemed Equip Worksheet										
Total TM Room Fixtures Cost										

continued . . .

. . . continued from page 42

COST CATEGORY	LABOR			EQUIP/MTRL		OTHER COST	TOTAL COST	AMORTIZATION		
	HOURS	RATE	COST	COST	SHIP			LIFE	SALVAGE	COST/YR
TRAINING										
Telemedicine Operation										
Telemedicine Maintenance/Support										
Medical Training										
Develop Training Plan										
Total Training Cost										
Total of Capital Costs										

Figure C–2c. Detailed Cost Estimation Model—Telemedicine Operating Costs

TM SYSTEM OPERATING COST	LABOR			EQUIP/MTRL/SUPPLIES		OTHER COST ($/yr)	TOTAL COST ($/yr)
	HOURS/MO	RATE ($/hr)	COST ($/yr)	COST ($/yr)	SHIP ($/yr)		
Personnel							
Medical Supplies							
Office Supplies							
Total System Operating Cost							

COMMUNICATIONS COST	COST		MINUTES/ MONTH	EQUIP/MTRL/SUPPLIES		OTHER COST ($/yr)	TOTAL COST ($/yr)
	($/Month)	($/Minute)		COST ($/yr)	SHIP ($/yr)		
Data/Video Communications							
Telephone							
Modem							
Fax							
E-mail/Internet							
Pager							
Other							
Total Communications Cost							

continued . . .

. . . continued from page 44

MAINTENANCE/SUPPORT COSTS	LABOR			EQUIP/MTRL/SUPPLIES		OTHER COST ($/yr)	TOTAL COST ($/yr)
	HOURS/MO	RATE ($/hr)	COST ($/yr)	COST ($/yr)	SHIP ($/yr)		
Support Subcontract							
Maintenance/Support Labor							
Spare Parts							
Other Support Equip/Material							
Total Maintenance Support Costs							
Total Operating Cost/Year							

Figure C–2d. Detailed Cost Estimation Model—Medical Personnel Costs

MAINTENANCE/SUPPORT COSTS (List by Medical Specialty)	CONSULT (MINUTES)	CONSULT-COST/HOUR		CONSULT-COST/CONSULT		OTHER COST ($/yr)	TOTAL COST ($/yr)
		$/hr	CONSULT/YR	$/CONSULT	CONSULT/YR		
Psychiatry							
Total Psychiatry Cost							
Dermatology							
Total Dermatology Cost							
Orthopedics							
Total Orthopedics Cost							
Other Specialties							
Total Other Specialties Cost							
Total Medical Personnel Cost/Year							

Figure C–2e. Detailed Cost Estimation Model—Medical Costs Avoided by Telemedicine

MEDICAL PERSONNEL (List by Medical Specialty)	CONSULT (MINUTES)	CONSULT-COST/HOUR		CONSULT-COST/CONSULT		OTHER COST ($/yr)	TOTAL COST ($/yr)
		$/hr	CONSULT/YR	$/CONSULT	CONSULT/YR		
Internal Consultations							
Total Internal Consultations Cost							
Local External Consultations							
Total External Consultations Cost							
Medical Center Consultations							
Total Medical Center Consultations Cost							
Total Medical Cost/Yr							

Figure C–2f. Detailed Cost Estimation Model—Medical Escort and Transport Costs Avoided

COST CATEGORY	LABOR COST/TRANSPORT or ESCORT					TRANSP $ ($/Trans)	OTHER $/ TRANSP-ESC	TRANSP ESCORT/YR	TOTAL COST ($/yr)
	HRS	RATE	OT HRS	OT RATE	LABOR COST				
INTERNAL CONSULTATIONS									
Administrative Personnel									
Medical Personnel									
Security Personnel									
Other Personnel									
Total Internal Consults Cost									
LOCAL EXTERNAL CONSULTATIONS									
Administrative Personnel									
Medical Personnel									
Security Personnel									
Other Personnel									
Escort Vehicle Cost									
Transport Vehicle Cost									
Ambulance Cost									
Total External Consults Cost									
MEDICAL CENTER CONSULTATIONS									
Administrative Personnel									
Medical Personnel									
Security Personnel									
Other Personnel									
Escort Vehicle Cost									
Ambulance Cost									
Charter Airflight									
Commercial Airline									
Total Medical Center Consultations Cost									
Total Escort/Transport Cost									

Figure C–2g. Detailed Cost Estimation Model—Telemedicine Installation Worksheet

COST CATEGORY	LABOR			MATERIAL		OTHER COST	TOTAL COST
	HOURS	RATE	COST	COST	SHIP		
System Integrator							
General							
Electronics							
Electrical							
Masonry/Plaster/Drywall							
Plumbing							
Painting							
Other—Carpet							
—Acoustic							
—Lighting							
Total Installation Cost							

Figure C–2h. Detailed Cost Estimation Model—Telemedicine Equipment Worksheet

ITEM DESCRIPTION	MANUFACTURER	PART NUMBER	QTY	UNIT COST	ITEM COSTS	SHIP COST	TOTAL COST
Telemedicine System							
Computer							
CODEC							
Display							
Cameras							
Medical Devices							
Consoles/Cabinets							
Other							
Total Telemedicine System Cost							

continued . . .

. . . continued from page 50

ITEM DESCRIPTION	MANUFACTURER	PART NUMBER	QTY	UNIT COST	ITEM COST	SHIP COST	TOTAL COST
Network/Communications							
Total Network/Comm Equip Cost							
Telemedicine Room Fixtures							
Total Telemedicine Room Fixtures Cost							
Total Telemedicine Equipment Cost/Yr							

Telemedicine system operating cost. This is the cost of the supplies and personnel services needed to operate the telemedicine room. To maintain accurate cost information for calculating costs and benefits, a consistent approach should be followed for cost entry here and on the Medical Costs Avoided by Telemedicine sheet (figure C–2e). Either one of the following approaches is satisfactory:

- Enter all costs for maintaining the telemedicine room. On the Medical Costs Avoided by Telemedicine sheet, enter in the Other Cost column the savings that accrue by replacing conventional care with telemedicine.

- Enter only those costs that are unique to telemedicine.

Communications cost. Space is provided in figure C–2c to enter all communications costs. However, the comments made above for cost entry also apply here. The data and video communications cost should be calculated accurately because it will be the largest operating cost item. Depending on the communications protocol you are using and your service provider, your data and video communications cost could be based on rate per minute per line, rate per minute for your selected bandwidth, rate per data packet (with or without a fixed monthly cost), or some combination of these rates. The model includes a contingency factor of 20 percent for estimating the cost of communications.

Maintenance and support costs. This is the cost for maintaining the telemedicine and communications equipment. If you have a fixed-cost support subcontract, enter the cost of that contract in the Other Cost column (figure C–2c). If you are providing maintenance, enter your labor, parts, and other support costs in the spaces provided.

Medical personnel costs

The Medical Personnel Costs sheet (figure C–2d) is used to calculate the cost for all personnel who provide medical services. Medical personnel should be listed by their specialty. Provisions are made for entering cost data for consultations where the cost is determined either on an hourly basis or on a per-consultation basis. The Consult (Minutes) column must be filled in for both cost methods. Note that the total consultation minutes per year are calculated for each physician on the basis of the Consult (Minutes) column entry. The total consultation time for all physicians is used to calculate communications costs.

Medical costs avoided by telemedicine

Theoretically, for each consultation performed through telemedicine, the cost of a conventional consultation should be avoided. You should review medical records for the past year and determine which patients could have been cared for through telemedicine. This will form the basis for establishing the number of telemedicine consultations that would have occurred over the same time period, as well as the number of internal, local external, and medical center consultations that could have been avoided through telemedicine. The medical specialties involved and your cost to provide these specialty services should be entered in the appropriate locations.

One of the most difficult tasks will be to establish an accurate count of external and medical center consultations avoided through telemedicine. If telemedicine provides better access to medical services or access to medical specialties that were otherwise not available, you may find that the more immediate treatments enabled by telemedicine reduce the incidents requiring transport of a patient for outside medical services. (Review the findings of the telemedicine demonstration project at http://www. ncjrs.org/telemedicine/toc.html for guidance.)

Medical escort and transport costs avoided

The Medical Escort and Transport Costs Avoided sheet (figure C–2f) is used to calculate the cost

avoided because patients treated through telemedicine did not require escort or transport. The cost categories list personnel normally involved in escorting or transporting patients. For external and medical center consultations, provisions are made to enter the cost to provide the transportation.

For internal medical consultations, escort costs may be avoided if the escort provided is part of the routine movement of inmates. For external and medical center consultations, enter the cost for planning, preparing paperwork, coordinating with the outside facility, and transporting the patient; travel time to and from the destination, time spent at the destination, and time for closing the incident; and all transportation costs.

Telemedicine installation worksheet

The Telemedicine Installation Worksheet (figure C–2g) provides additional space for entering cost data for installing the telemedicine system. No entries are required on this worksheet if all installation costs were entered on the Capital Costs sheet. Cost information entered on the Telemedicine Installation Worksheet will be automatically transferred to the Capital Costs sheet if you are using the electronic version.

Telemedicine equipment worksheet

The Telemedicine Equipment Worksheet (figure C–2h) provides additional space for entering cost data for procuring the telemedicine equipment. No entries are required on this worksheet if all equipment costs were entered on the Capital Costs sheet. Cost information entered on the Telemedicine Equipment Worksheet will be automatically transferred to the Capital Costs sheet if you are using the electronic version.

Appendix D
Medical Requirements Analysis Worksheet

Medical Requirements Analysis

Construct a form or worksheet to collect the information outlined below. Information should be gathered for external outpatient consultation, external inpatient consultation, and internal consultation. This information should be gathered for each subspecialty, such as dermatology, orthopedics, or cardiology.

- The number of routine consultations.

- The number of emergency consultations.

- Frequency of consultations (patients seen per month).

- Locations consultations are conducted.

- Monthly costs.

- Number of consultations appropriate for telemedicine (case examples).

- Time required for consultations.

- Total monthly time required for consultations.

- Type of data used.
  - Static or dynamic images, textual.
  - Source of data (x-ray, EKG strip, etc.).
  - How often will data be produced?
  - How often will data be recalled for later use?
  - How often will data be communicated to a remote location?
  - How many locations?
  - Expectations of data (image quality, annotations).
  - Format of data for presentation (color, printed, viewed).
  - Response time for data (prison-telecom-hospital).

- Equipment used for consultations.

- Number of inmates on waiting list.

- Factors causing wait list.

- Current practices and procedures for medical consultation.

Appendix E

**Medical Requirements Analysis—
Clinic Survey Form**

Medical Requirements Analysis—Clinic Survey Form

For planning purposes, responses to the following questions should be gathered from the clinics.

A. What telemedicine clinics would you like to see scheduled at your facility? Please specify any other clinics that are not listed below:

SPECIALTY REQUIRED	FREQUENCY OF CLINIC (WEEKLY, MONTHLY, ETC.)	NO. OF PATIENTS PER CLINIC	WEEKDAY CHOICES			
			1ST	2ND	3RD	HOURS
1. Psychiatry						
2. Dermatology						
3. Orthopedics						
4. Podiatry						
5. Cardiology						
6.						
7.						
8.						

B. What specialty areas would you like to have available for nonclinic consultations (nonemergency)?

1. _____

2. _____

3. _____

4. _____

5. _____

6. _____

7. _____

8. _____

C. How quickly would you need to have the nonclinic consultations (nonemergency)?

> All specialty areas have the same response time, _____business days.
>
> or
>
> The maximum response time varies by specialty area, as follows:

SPECIALTY AREA	MAXIMUM RESPONSE TIME FOR SCHEDULING CONSULTATIONS
1.	
2.	
3.	
4.	
5.	
6.	
7.	
8.	

D. What turnaround time is required for teleradiology consultations for plain films? _____ business days.

Initially, would a faxed consultation report meet your needs? _____ Yes   _____ No

How soon should the hardcopy consultation report follow?   _____ business days.

E. Is the number of plain films you indicated equal to the number of monthly teleradiology consultations, or is the number of monthly consultations less than this number? In other words, how many monthly teleradiology consultations do you project and how many monthly films do you project?

> _____ monthly teleradiology consultations.   _____ monthly films.

F. Other comments:

_____

_____

_____

_____

_____

Appendix F

Position Description—
Telemedicine Coordinator

Introduction

The incumbent serves as the telemedicine coordinator at a prison remote telemedicine site. Services are coordinated in collaboration with the off-site telemedicine consultant and the prison staff. The telemedicine coordinator is primarily responsible for coordinating telemedicine operations and medical consultations and for providing training and assistance for the prison medical staff.

Major Duties

- Serves as the telemedicine coordinator at a remote prison telemedicine site.

- Coordinates and schedules subspecialty consultations (clinic and nonclinic) for inmate medical care with the telemedicine consultants. Operates telemedicine equipment during telemedicine consultations (as appropriate) and helps the presenter use the telemedicine equipment during the telemedicine consultation.

- Assembles patient consultation forms and medical records for faxing or mailing to telemedicine consultant before the scheduled subspecialty clinics. Reviews information in advance to ensure completeness and legibility.

- Collects and reports required patient evaluation data on a timely basis.

- Ensures telemedicine equipment is fully operational and maintained and is properly set up and tested before scheduled consultations.

- Maintains stock of supplies and ensures security of the exam room and equipment.

- Provides reports and status updates as required.

- Provides input for developing telemedicine policy and procedure.

- Teaches other health care personnel to operate and maintain the telemedicine equipment.

- Works responsibly and cooperatively with entire telemedicine team.

- Ensures patients' privacy and confidentiality.

- Performs related duties as required, but accepts only those duties that are commensurate with educational preparation, training, experience, and licensing laws.

- Adheres to all infection-control policies and procedures.

- Is subject to prison security background check, which is to include urinalysis drug screen.

Knowledge Required

- Working knowledge of medical theory, clinical practice and patient care, and medical terminology.

- Working knowledge of the use of computers, associated software applications, office equipment, and medical equipment (e.g., stethoscope).

- Excellent interpersonal skills.

- Ability to understand medical records and accurately extract and enter patient data from patient encounters.

- Familiarity with prison custody, safety, and security regulations; health service policies and procedures; and inmate behavior.

- Ability to train other health care staff to operate and maintain the telemedicine equipment.

- Knowledgeable in the legal and ethical aspects of correctional medicine.

Supervisory Controls

The position is supervised by the head of Health Services. However, the incumbent performs effectively and independently. The incumbent will have the ability to set priorities, to be organized, and to determine when to seek appropriate assistance. The prison warden will have ultimate authority and responsibility for all telemedicine activities and efforts at the prison remote site. The incumbent will be guided by the needs of the prison in all tasks performed.

Physical Demands

This position may require long periods of standing or sitting. The incumbent is required to lift and move supplies and to use specific medical equipment. The incumbent must be able to function under stressful circumstances and be capable of coping with complex or rapidly changing situations.

Work Environment

The incumbent works in a hazardous-duty environment in a correctional setting. In addition, this individual is subject to all exposures common to the health care setting, including infectious and communicable diseases, irritant chemicals, and electrical hazards. The incumbent does not provide direct patient care.

Appendix G

Developing Telemedicine Procedures

A successful telemedicine consult requires the consultant physician or other health care provider to be thoroughly prepared. Before the consult, the originating provider should review and collect information relevant to the consultation. The health care provider should have established procedures for collecting information for telemedicine consultations.

This publication does not identify and develop procedures for all specialty requirements. Rather it presents guidance on how to develop procedures that can be used to conduct telemedicine consultations.

Any procedures developed must be consistent with acceptable medical practices. Competent medical personnel must review the procedures on a regular basis.

Procedures should be developed for various medical specialties that require different information and different preparation. A cardiology consult may require information on recent stress tests, for example, while a dermatology clinic may require the results of specified lab tests. Procedures for dermatology consults can be established by asking the consulting dermatologist for the information necessary to conduct a telemedicine consult. With guidance from the consulting dermatologist, a written procedure can be designed to be used during a dermatology consult. The same process can be used to create procedures for other medical specialties.

Any information the provider would have available for an in-office patient should be provided to the telemedicine consultant. The patient's medical record and any relevant tests or laboratory results must be available. In some cases, this information must be transmitted to the consulting physician before the consult.

State medical boards may be able to provide information on State laws and regulations pertaining to telemedicine. The boards of specific medical specialties may also be helpful, as may other correctional agencies that have established telemedicine programs. For example, the Federal prison system has an established telemedicine program and procedures for conducting telemedicine consults. For copies of its procedures, contact—

Assistant Director
Health Services Division
Federal Bureau of Prisons
320 First Street N.W.
Washington, DC 20534
http://www.bop.gov

Other contacts that may be helpful in developing procedures for conducting a telemedicine consult include—

National Commission on Correctional
    Health Care
1300 West Belmont Avenue
Chicago, IL 60651
http://www.ncchc.org

American Telemedicine Association
910 17th Street N.W.
Suite 314
Washington, DC 20006
http://www.atmeda.org

Appendix H

Glossary of Telemedicine Terms

ACR-NEMA. American College of Radiology and National Equipment Manufacturers Association. These organizations have jointly developed standards for teleradiology practice. For computed tomography (CT), magnetic resonance imaging (MRI), ultrasound, nuclear medicine, and digital fluoroscopy, images must be scanned at a resolution of 500 pixels x 500 lines at a depth of 8 bits (256 *gray scale*) or better; for diagnostic x-rays, 2,000 pixels x 2,000 lines ("2k by 2k") at 12 bits (4,096 gray scale).

ADSL. Asymmetric digital subscriber line. A system currently under trial in several metropolitan areas. Uses existing copper phone lines. With proper retooling by telephone companies, ADSL can supply 6-Mbps downstream delivery of data.

algorithm. A mathematical coding scheme. A coding scheme can compress digitized broadband video or audio signals so that the signals can be transmitted over a lower (and less expensive) *bandwidth.* Standards-based algorithms enable communications with standards-based systems from disparate manufacturers. Proprietary algorithms are unique to individual manufacturers and enable communications only between equipment from that manufacturer. Current practice strongly encourages standards-based systems.

analog. Information (electronic or otherwise) that is created and transmitted as a continuous stream. Waveforms (e.g., on oscilloscopes) are analog. Compare this to *digital* information generated by computers. Modems are used to convert digital computer data to analog form for sending over standard (plain old telephone system, *POTS*) lines.

annotation. The capability to add comments or highlights to captured or live video. Simultaneous shared annotation of captured (or, less commonly, live video) images allows conference participants to clearly point out the areas in question on an image, and may provide significant instructional value.

ATM. Asynchronous transfer mode. A telecommunications service that supports switched multimedia communications from T1 (1.544 *Mbps*) to very high data rates (155 Mbps and higher). Not commonly available.

audio-only conference add-ins. The capability to add another site into a videoconference using only an audio connection. This feature uses a regular phone line connected to the *CODEC* to connect someone who is not near a video site but needs to be part of the conversation.

bandwidth. The capacity of an electronic transmission medium to transmit data per unit of time. The higher the bandwidth, the more data can be transmitted. Typically measured in kilobits or megabits per second. Standard telephones are low-bandwidth devices (a maximum bandwidth of 33.6 *Kbps*). Cable television uses high bandwidth (up to 140 *Mbps*).

beam splitter. A device for tele-otoscopes or -ophthalmoscopes that allows the clinician to see directly into the eye or ear and also routes a portion of the image to the video camera. This capability is usually preferred by the clinician, who is accustomed to looking directly through the device rather than at a video monitor.

bit. Binary digit. The basic 0–1 unit of information used by computers for information entry, storage, and transmission. Data rates in telecommunications are often referred to in bits (b) per second. See *bandwidth, byte, Kbps, Mbps.*

BRI. Basic rate interface.

bursty data. Short, intense transmissions of grouped, related information. Sometimes called "boluses of data" by medical clinicians.

byte. The amount of computer memory needed to store one character. Each data character, such as the letter A, is composed of 8 *bits*, called a byte (abbreviated B). Units of storage are often referred to in terms of the number of bytes (e.g., "100-MB hard drive").

camera control. The capability to control the video camera used in the consultation, either at the near end (local control of local pan-tilt-zoom iris-focus) or the far end (hub control of pan-tilt-zoom at the remote site). This feature may be quite useful in consultations if the examiner wants to control the remote camera's view without having to provide verbal directions to the assistant at the remote site.

CCD. Charge-coupled device. An integrated circuit, or "chip." A 1-CCD (one-chip) camera contains a single charge-coupled device with specialized semi-conductors containing photosensitive cells that generate voltage when struck by photons of light. One photosensitive cell equates to one pixel in the displayed image. The number of cells on a chip determines the number of *pixels* of resolution that the camera can display. The larger the chip, the greater the image resolution. Increased resolution is accomplished either by using larger chips or by using more chips. Single-chip cameras do a good job. Two-chip cameras use one chip for *chrominance* and one for *luminence*. Three-chip cameras do an even better job, because they have more total cells and because they use one chip each to capture red, green, and blue light. Three-chip cameras provide images with higher resolution and better color representation, and can cost 10 times as much as single-chip cameras. CCD scanners for teleradiology are less expensive than laser scanners and may not have the same ability to detect contrast. This may

or may not affect their ability to transmit diagnostic-quality images.

chip. An integrated circuit. See *CCD*.

chrominance. Hue and saturation (color) on a video monitor.

CIF. Common intermediate format. An international standard for video display formats developed by the *TSS* (see *ITU-T Standards*).

CODEC. Coder/decoder hardware or software used with interactive video systems that converts an *analog* signal to *digital*, then compresses it so that lower *bandwidth* telecommunications lines can be used. The signal is decompressed and converted back to analog output by a compatible CODEC at the receiving end. The compression method (*algorithm*) may be proprietary or standards based.

CSU/DSU. Channel service unit/data service unit. A hardware device that is needed to terminate a high-speed telecommunications connection. It is inserted between the *telemedicine* system (e.g., *CODEC*) and the communications line. The device conditions and strengthens the signal and supports the necessary link protocols for transmission of data over leased or switched communications lines. It also acts as a *multiplexer*.

DICOM. Digital imaging and communications in medicine. An industry standard for connection of, and communications among, medical imaging devices. The most recent iteration is DICOM 3.

digital. Information coded in discrete numerical values (*bits*). Digital data streams are less susceptible to interference than *analog* data streams. Also, because they are made up of zeros and ones (bits), they can be manipulated and integrated easily with other data streams (voice, video, data).

digital camera. A camera that captures images (still or motion) digitally and does not require *analog*-to-*digital* conversion before the image can be transmitted or stored in a computer. The analog-to-digital conversion process (which takes place in a *CODEC*) usually causes some degradation of the image and a time delay in transmission. Avoiding this step theoretically provides a better, faster image at the receiving end.

DS3. A *leased line* (nonswitched) running at 45 *Mbps.* Compare with *OC3, T1, ISDN.*

duplex audio. A communications mode that enables simultaneous transmission and reception of audio signals in both directions. Full-duplex audio enables both ends of a conference to speak and be heard simultaneously (like a regular telephone call). Half-duplex audio supports only one site speaking at a time; other speakers will be cut off.

echo cancellation. A feature that prevents a system from picking up the sound from its own speakers and transmitting it back to other conference sites. Highly desirable for acceptable audioconferencing.

encryption. A security feature that ensures that only the parties who are supposed to be participating in a video conference or data transfer are able to do so. It is accomplished by mathematically transposing a file or data stream so that it cannot be deciphered at the receiving end without the proper key.

Ethernet. A local area *network* datalink protocol operating at 10 *Mbps* to 100 Mbps.

firewall. A computer connected to both the Internet and the local hospital information *network* that prevents the passing of Internet traffic to the internal hospital network. It provides an added layer of protection against computer hackers.

fps. Frames per second. See *frame rate.*

frame rate. The number of frames per second (*fps*) displayed on a video monitor. A frame rate of 25–30 fps is considered "full motion"; most broadcast video operates at this rate. A frame rate of 15 fps is noticeably "jerky." Slower frame rates may be inadequate for observing and analyzing gait and motion.

frame relay. A service that supports data rates in the range of 56 *Kbps* to 1.54 *Mbps.* The frame relay circuit often comes in different levels of committed information rates. Regional telephone companies can offer frame relay cheaper because they can oversubscribe these circuits to users and share the *bandwidth.*

freeze-frame video. A video camera feature that allows the consultant to get a well-framed and focused still image of a lesion or other medical condition for closer examination. Still images captured from a live video source are often of higher resolution than the live video picture and, as a result, may provide more diagnostic value. Also referred to as *image capture.*

frequency response. A relative measure of audio quality, expressed in cycles per second, or hertz (Hz). Generally, the broader the frequency response, the better the signal. To approximate a standard acoustic stethoscope, an electronic stethoscope should be able to send and receive sounds as low as 30 Hz (for low-pitched heart murmurs) and as high as 1,000 Hz (for squeaks, wheezes, and pops heard in lung conditions). Many electronic stethoscopes can have their frequency response optimized for either heart or lung sounds by flipping a switch.

full-motion video. Video that runs at 25 or 30 frames per second, down to a minimum of 10–15 *fps.* Any frame rate less than about 10 fps is approaching *slow-scan video.*

ghosting. A motion artifact in monitor displays of compressed video images. As an image moves quickly across the field of view (e.g., an arm waving), it leaves a trail of ghost images that resolve as the movement stops.

graphic equalizer. A device that allows the user to emphasize or deemphasize selected frequencies within an audio sample. An example is the different settings for heart and lung sounds in electronic stethoscopes. See *frequency response.*

graphics stand. A device that is typically used to support a document so that images of graphics or text can be captured and transmitted. Can be used for skin lesions and the like.

gray scale. The levels (shades) of gray that a screen or *pixel* within a screen can display.

GUI. Graphical user interface. See *interface.*

H.230, H.242, H.256, H.263, H.324, ... See *ITU–T Standards, video format.*

IATV. Interactive televideo. Also abbreviated *ITV.*

image capture. See *freeze-frame video.*

image management. The capability to sort, arrange, and manipulate stored images into functional groups. Systems without this feature allow the user to store images only in the order in which they were saved; once stored, they cannot be rearranged.

INMARSAT. An international global telecommunications satellite *network,* established by government treaty in 1979, with 79 member countries. Land Earth Stations (fixed or portable, even to size) provide links between rural sites and telecommunications networks. INMARSAT can provide low-*bandwidth digital* services anywhere on the Earth's surface for as little as $1 per minute.

integrator. A vendor that uses parts from other manufacturers to produce a product that is optimal for the particular user's requirements.

interface. The means whereby a system enables information to be accessed and modified. A graphical user interface with mouse-controlled, point-and-click on-screen icons is an example of an easy-to-use interface device.

ISDN. Integrated services digital network. A low- to medium-speed technology for digital telephony. Usually transmits at 64–128 *Kbps,* although higher speeds are possible.

ISO. International Organization for Standardization. The ISO, in conjunction with the International Electrotechnical Commission, establishes and coordinates worldwide standards for, among other things, electronic information exchange.

ISP. Internet service provider. The local, regional, or national company that provides dial-up connections to the Internet, as well as hosting of home pages.

ITU–T. International Telecommunications Union–Telecommunications Standardization Sector (*TSS*). An organization founded in 1865 as a telegraphy standards body and now is a United Nations agency.

ITU–T Standards. The H series refers to videoconferencing standards; the G series, to audioconferencing standards; and the T series, to data transfer standards. The *T.120* series, in particular, refers to *image capture, annotation,* and transfer in videoconferences.

ITV. Interactive televideo. Also abbreviated *IATV.*

JPEG. Joint Photographic Experts Group. The international group that has developed standards for still-image compression.

KB. Kilobyte. 1,024 bits of data.

Kbps. Kilobits (thousands of bits) per second. A typical compressed-video clinical interaction is transmitted at 385 Kbps.

LAN. Local area network. A computer network linking computers, printers, servers, and other equipment within an organization.

laser digitizer. A scanner that uses a laser device to capture image information in *digital* form. Very high resolution and wide *gray-scale* range are possible.

leased line. A point-to-point private line for the sole use of the party who leases the circuit. Unlike a *switched line*, the price of a leased line does not vary as a function of usage.

leveling. A software manipulation technique, using mathematical *algorithms,* to compensate for a tele-radiology monitor's inability to provide the same contrast and bit depth as the original hardcopy x-ray. This feature provides much more usable clinical information.

low-pass filter. A filter for leveling out the borders in the screen display of a radiology image.

luminence. Characteristics of brightness for a video monitor.

MB. Megabytes (millions of *bytes*).

Mbps. Megabits (millions of *bits*) per second. A typical uncompressed video signal requires 45 Mbps (or more) to transmit.

modem. Modulator-demodulator. A device that enables transmission of *digital* data (by transforming it to and from *analog* waveforms) over standard analog phone lines and cable video systems.

MPEG. Moving Picture Experts Group. A group of standards for compressing and storing motion video.

MRI. Magnetic resonance imaging.

multiplexer. A hardware device that combines two or more subchannels of information for transmission as a single data stream.

MUX. *Multiplexer.*

network. An assortment of electronic devices (computers, printers, scanners, etc.) connected (by wires or wireless) for mutual exchange of *digital* information.

ocular tube adapter. A device that allows a camera to be mounted to any microscope. This feature is needed to adapt a telepathology system to an existing ocular microscope without a camera port. Capturing images through an ocular tube has some disadvantages that must be weighed against the cost of a new scope.

OC3. A high-speed *digital* transmission capability of 1.55 *Mbps.* Compare with *DS3, T1, ISDN.*

PBX. Private branch exchange. A telephone switch, typically located at the customer site, connected to the public telephone *network* but operated by the customer. PBXs may be *digital* or *analog.*

peripheral device. An attachment to a videoconferencing system to augment its communications or medical capabilities. Examples include electronic stethoscopes, otoscopes, ophthalmoscopes, derma-scopes, graphic stands, and scanners.

PIP. Picture in picture. This feature allows both ends of the videoconference to be viewed simultaneously on a single monitor. PIP swap allows the user to switch the two video pictures so that the local video fills the largest portion of the screen.

pixel. The smallest unit of a *raster* display; a picture cell with specific color or brightness. The more pixels an image has, the more detail, or resolution, it can display.

POTS. Plain old telephone system. The *analog,* public switched telephone *network* in common use throughout the world. POTS enables voice phone calls and data transmission of up to 56 *Kbps,* as well as limited videoconferencing.

PRI. Primary rate interface.

primary user interface device. The device used to control the videoconferencing system. Hardwired and wireless, keyboard, mouse, and touchscreen options each have advantages and disadvantages. The user should seriously consider in what setting and for what application the system will be used to determine the preferred *interface.*

printer interface. A device that allows data and images sent or received via the computer to be sent to a printer. This enables reports, images, and data shared in a videoconference to be rendered as hardcopy for recordkeeping and teaching purposes.

raster. A pattern of scanning lines covering the area upon which the image is projected in the cathode ray tube of a television set.

real time. Transmission and reception of audio, video, and data virtually simultaneously (without more than a fraction of a second delay). Applications that are transmitted within a few seconds are sometimes called "near" real time. Compare with *store-and-forward, slow-scan video.*

resolution. The level of detail that can be captured or displayed. For video displays (*teleradiology* or interactive video), resolution is measured in *pixels* x lines x *bit* depth.

RGB. Red green blue. A coding language that controls the electron gun in cathode ray tube monitors. The video signal that enters the monitor is separated into its component parts and converted to RGB; the video images are then rendered on the monitor's screen.

rollabout unit. A portable teleconferencing or *telemedicine* system in which the monitor, *CODEC,* camera, etc., are placed in a cabinet with wheels that can be rolled from room to room. "Rollabout" can be a misleading term, because some units weigh more than 500 pounds and are very cumbersome to move.

room unit. A stationary teleconferencing or telemedicine system, usually with two large monitors, that is placed more or less permanently at a single site.

RS–232. An interface between data terminal equipment and data communications equipment, using serial binary data exchange.

scan line. *Raster.*

slow-scan video. A slow progression of freeze-frames (less than 1 or 2 per second). Also called "still video." Compare with *full-motion video.*

spooling. The capability to review one image or data set, while receiving and storing additional images for subsequent review without "locking up" the computer.

store-and-forward. Captured audio clips, video clips, still images, or data that are transmitted or received at a later time (sometimes no more than a minute later). Compare with *real time.*

switched line or **network.** A telecommunications mode similar to a dial-up telephone line. There is often a usage charge for switched services, particularly for long-distance connections, such as telephone lines. Compare with *leased line,* where the connection is continuously open and charges are usually levied at a flat, monthly rate.

Switched 56. A dial-up 56-*Kbps* digital line, billed at a monthly rate plus a per-minute charge, as with a *POTS* phone line. Costs for switched 56 service vary from provider to provider, but generally are about the same or somewhat more than those of a voice call.

T1. A leased line providing 1.544-*Mbps* data. T1 is available almost everywhere and can be fractionated. Fractional T1 services are less expensive than full T1. Typical interactive video *telemedicine* programs transmit video images at "1/4 T1" rates (384 *Kbps*).

T.120. A standard for audio and graphics exchanges, supporting higher resolutions and pointing and *annotation* (which the H.320 standard does not).

tariff. Telecommunications rates set by either a Federal or State regulatory body.

TCP/IP. Transmission control protocol/Internet protocol. The most popular open-standard protocols used in data *networks* today. The Internet protocol is used to route packets of data on a network.

telemedicine. The provision of health care over a distance using telecommunications technology.

teleradiology. The interpretation of diagnostic images sent over a distance using leased or switched transmission lines.

third-party equipment. Equipment added to an existing system to expand the original system's capabilities. Some vendors modify videoconferencing systems with additional cameras to fabricate a *telemedicine* capability. Third-party equipment may not be covered by the vendor's warranty, and its performance may not be guaranteed.

transmission rate. The amount of information per unit of time that a technology such as a conventional (*POTS*) or *digital* (*ISDN* or *T1*) telephone line, satellite or wireless telecommunications, or *LAN* can transmit. A typical *POTS*-based *modem* can transmit 33.6 *Kbps* of information per second.

TSS. Telecommunications Standardization Sector of the International Telecommunications Union. See *ITU-T.*

twisted pair. A pair of copper wires that has been twisted to minimize electronic interference. Standard telephone wire.

URL. Universal resource locator. The World Wide Web address (typically in the form: http://www.name_of_site) of an Internet home page or other document.

video format. The manner by which video images are exchanged between the remote and hub sites. Formats include National Television System Committee (NTSC), phase alternation line (PAL), high-definition television (HDTV), and sequential color and memory (SECAM).

video on demand. The ability to provide instantaneous access to remotely stored sources of video.

video output. Composite, S-video.

videophone. A small, standalone video appliance with a small camera and circulation—not part of a computer or larger videoconferencing system—that enables interactive audio-video communications over *POTS* and *ISDN*.

WAN. Wide area *network*. A computer network wider in geographic scope than a *LAN*. Provides *digital* communications (voice, video, data) over switched (*ISDN*, *switched 56*) or unswitched (fractional *T1*, T1) networks.

About the National Institute of Justice

NIJ is the research and development agency of the U.S. Department of Justice and is the only Federal agency solely dedicated to researching crime control and justice issues. NIJ provides objective, independent, nonpartisan, evidence-based knowledge and tools to meet the challenges of crime and justice, particularly at the State and local levels. NIJ's principal authorities are derived from the Omnibus Crime Control and Safe Streets Act of 1968, as amended (42 U.S.C. §§ 3721–3722).

NIJ's Mission

In partnership with others, NIJ's mission is to prevent and reduce crime, improve law enforcement and the administration of justice, and promote public safety. By applying the disciplines of the social and physical sciences, NIJ—

- **Researches** the nature and impact of crime and delinquency.

- **Develops** applied technologies, standards, and tools for criminal justice practitioners.

- **Evaluates** existing programs and responses to crime.

- **Tests** innovative concepts and program models in the field.

- **Assists** policymakers, program partners, and justice agencies.

- **Disseminates** knowledge to many audiences.

NIJ's Strategic Direction and Program Areas

NIJ is committed to five challenges as part of its strategic plan: 1) **rethinking justice** and the processes that create just communities; 2) **understanding the nexus** between social conditions and crime; 3) **breaking the cycle** of crime by testing research-based interventions; 4) **creating the tools** and technologies that meet the needs of practitioners; and 5) **expanding horizons** through interdisciplinary and international perspectives. In addressing these strategic challenges, the Institute is involved in the following program areas: crime control and prevention, drugs and crime, justice systems and offender behavior, violence and victimization, communications and information technologies, critical incident response, investigative and forensic sciences (including DNA), less-than-lethal technologies, officer protection, education and training technologies, testing and standards, technology assistance to law enforcement and corrections agencies, field testing of promising programs, and international crime control. NIJ communicates its findings through conferences and print and electronic media.

NIJ's Structure

The NIJ Director is appointed by the President and confirmed by the Senate. The NIJ Director establishes the Institute's objectives, guided by the priorities of the Office of Justice Programs, the U.S. Department of Justice, and the needs of the field. NIJ actively solicits the views of criminal justice and other professionals and researchers to inform its search for the knowledge and tools to guide policy and practice.

NIJ has three operating units. The Office of Research and Evaluation manages social science research and evaluation and crime mapping research. The Office of Science and Technology manages technology research and development, standards development, and technology assistance to State and local law enforcement and corrections agencies. The Office of Development and Communications manages field tests of model programs, international research, and knowledge dissemination programs. NIJ is a component of the Office of Justice Programs, which also includes the Bureau of Justice Assistance, the Bureau of Justice Statistics, the Office of Juvenile Justice and Delinquency Prevention, and the Office for Victims of Crime.

To find out more about the National Institute of Justice, please contact:

National Criminal Justice Reference Service
P.O. Box 6000
Rockville, MD 20849–6000
800–851–3420
e-mail: *askncjrs@ncjrs.org*

To obtain an electronic version of this document, access the NIJ Web site
(http://www.ojp.usdoj.gov/nij).

If you have questions, call or e-mail NCJRS.